No Permission Required

BRINGING S.T.E.A.M. TO LIFE IN K-12 SCHOOLS

Susan M. Riley

No Permission Required: A Guide for Bringing S.T.E.A.M to Life

Published by Visionyst Press, an imprint of The Vision Board, LLC. 742 Charingworth Road, Westminster, MD 21158. http://thevisionboard.org

Printed in the United States of America. Cover art © 2014 by The Vision Board, LLC.

All web links and references in this book are correct as of the publication date below but may have become inactive or otherwise modified since that time. If you notice a deactivated or changed link or reference, please email visionystpress@thevisionboard.org with the words "update this link" in the subject line. In your message, please specify the web link, the book title and the page number on which the link appears.

All reference trademarks are the property of their respective owners.

ISBN: 978-0-692-02657-1
Library of Congress Control Number: 2014937528
Visionyst Press Printing: April 2014

Acknowledgements

This book would not have been possible without a great deal of support, insights, and learning opportunities provided for me by some incredible individuals and organizations. It with sincere gratitude and humility that I would like to thank:

Piney Grove Elementary, North Elementary and Walter Bracken STEAM Academy and their respective leaders highlighted throughout this book. The work of these schools, instructional teams, and leaders is incredible and their stories were an honor to share.

My wonderful STEAMteam Ambassadors! This group reviewed the book prior to its release, put in countless hours of providing me with valuable suggestions, and were passionate advocates of its message. My sincere thanks goes to: Betsy Randall-David, Brenda Cloyed, Kathy Grundei, Lynda Chick, Jennifer Kauffman, Leisa Dodson, Michelle Ridlen, Amanda Juhasz, Corinne Gettys, Brenda Keller, Mellissa Hunt, Leslie Lausten, Meredith Tateo, Susan Alexander, Jan Hennessy, Deborah Knispel, Deborah Gustlin, Kimberly Haynes, Kim Taylor Knight, Rebecca Engelman, Edward Varner, Amy McBroom, Jennifer Lane, Sandra Koberlein, Brianne DeFrang, Roberta Evans, Rebecca Williams and Mar Ollero.

Charlotte Smelser and Martha Menz, two of this country's finest leaders of professional development opportunities for all educators. Thank you for allowing me to brainstorm with you and for being a soundboard for my own learning and growth.

The Curriculum and Instruction team at Anne Arundel County Public Schools, especially Rotunda Floyd-Cooper, Ava Tasker-Mitchell, Skip Lee, and Patti Flores for helping me refine a clear definition of curriculum design and instruction that is meaningful for teaching and learning.

Andrea Kane and Greg Pilewski - I love our team! Here's to many more years of creative adventures together.

Kacey Smith - I consider myself blessed to have your unwavering support and friendship.

To my family: John, Ginger, Andrew, Diana, Warren, James, Art, Vickie, Aileen, Kim, Dave, Peyton and Connor for helping me to keep what is important a priority.

And as always, to my husband Kevin and my daughter Emma. Without you, my dreams wouldn't be possible and my reality wouldn't be my dreams.

table of contents

Are we really allowed to do this?

Standing in yet another school media center, I look around at the faces that are staring expectantly at me waiting for a response. Waiting for permission. And not believing it when the permission is so freely given. We have just spent an entire day discovering, unpacking, and weaving together arts integration and STEAM strategies; their excitement has only been tempered by this one question.

Are we really ALLOWED to do this?

This question has been holding these educators back all day and it's both frustrating and encouraging to watch. It's like watching a baby walk for the first time. When they look at you with that same question after taking one tentative step, you're dying for them to keep going and be set free from the tethers that have held them captive from exploring the world around them. And yet...they sit right back down.

Are we really allowed to do THIS?

For so long, educators have been shoved and pulled and constrained into a mold of what others wanted them to teach. Not only what others wanted them to teach, but also how and when and where so that the craft of teaching was all but automated. Pacing guides became the teachers. No questions, no ambiguity. Standardized teaching to match standardized tests to create standardized students.

So it's no wonder that educators are tentative when I waltz into their professional development days sharing strategies and lessons and assessments that encourage discovery, creativity and (dare I speak it's name) the arts. How will we ever test those? And if I am being held accountable to the test, certainly this kind of teaching isn't allowed since it would be impossible to test them in a standardized fashion. Does any of this sound familiar to you?

Here's the good news: you already have permission. As I explained to that group in the school media center, and to so many others who have asked me the exact same question, you are being asked to learn how to engage your students, increase their achievement and prepare them for the 21st century. And, if you are being sent to professional development sessions to learn about Arts Integration, STEAM, Project-Based Learning or Inquiry-Driven instruction, your administrators have invested in you to learn how to do this. Not only do you have permission, you are being expected to engage in this kind of teaching. That should be your baby-can-walk moment of clarity. What other permission are you looking for?

Even if you haven't been sent to a professional development session on those topics, my bet is that your school has been focused on 21st century skills, how to increase student engagement and achievement, and looking intensely at how teachers teach. All of these areas require that we shift from giving to guiding, in being able to unpack new standards and deliver instruction that meets those new demands and to assess our students based on their process and their products. You are certainly being given permission to do all of this - which is all based in artistic processes and practices. That's the whole point of this book: showing you how to authentically leverage these practices to integrate across content areas in ways that encourage exploration, creativity, and empowerment. We are on a journey towards gathering STEAM and this book will show you the pathways to getting there.

Many educators are simply waiting for their administrators or supervisors to step up and say, "this is okay" and to be given the latitude to try some of the incredible ideas and lessons they read about or watch from others. And while some supervisors may be as explicit as this, many will not. Many will send you to a training and then expect you as a professional to apply what you have learned. This may be all the permission you receive, but it is enough. Take it and run, and never look back. But there's one more thing you need to know before you go:

There is no permission required to teach like an artist.

- You don't need to ask if it's okay to engage your students through integrated learning.

- You don't need to ask if it's okay to use the arts to access the whole mind of a child.

- You don't need to ask if it's okay to bring relevance and vigor and passion and discovery into your classroom.

- You don't need to ask if it's okay to get out of the way of the learning process and encourage collaboration.

Why? Because all of these are attributes of classrooms where students are successful. All of these things are what great teachers do and what everyone wants for their own children to experience. If you are teaching this way, your students will have success and will achieve to their greatest potential. And, your students are doing this all anyway, with or without you. No permission required.

So stop asking for it! Stop waiting for someone to tell you that you are allowed to move beyond the script or to take the time to explore an integrated lesson. There is plenty of data and studies to support that integrated learning boosts student achievement and makes learning more meaningful. So be like Nike™ and just do it! Dive in and take a chance that this type of teaching may just be what opens the door for your students. They certainly aren't asking permission for how they learn. It's time we all stopped asking permission for how to teach and instead focus on taking intentional actions for meeting each of their unique needs. It's time to let go and walk, baby.

How to Use this Resource

This book is intended to be used as a practical guide for reference, implementation and support of STEAM initiatives. It is broken into three large subsections which can be read in order, or used alone to unpack the complexities of this approach. While you don't *need* to work through this book in order, it is advised that you ingest and digest all of it comprehensively before implementing a long-term plan for STEAM in your classroom or school. Each section can stand alone, but is more powerful when used in conjunction with the other parts of the book. Additionally, you will find 3 distinctly different approaches to STEAM in case studies from schools around the United States that share both the opportunities and the obstacles that many face in this endeavor. These are interspersed throughout Parts 1 and 2 as a way for you to see the practical applications of the STEAM design.

Part one is a focus on the what and why of STEAM. Here, you'll find key definitions, an understanding of not only the "what" of STEAM but also the process behind this approach, and practical strategies that can be used as a driver for integrated lessons and units. This section is intended to provide a solid foundation in STEAM models and applications to support the work of building or extending a school initiative.

Part two builds upon the strategies presented in part one and uses them to showcase the how of STEAM. In this section, you'll discover how to take the practices in part one and embed them authentically into the curriculum planning process. We will dig deeply into what STEAM looks like, what behaviors are present in a high-functioning STEAM initiative, how to build an environment within the school that captures the essence of these practices and embedding the STEAM process and strategies into the curriculum throughout its cycle of development.

Part three is your starter guide for the strategies presented in parts one and two. Here, you'll find full sample lessons with grade band extensions for each of the STEAM strategies highlighted, as well as aligned assessments for each lesson. Each lesson is aligned to either the Common Core State Standards in Mathematics, the Next Generation Science Standards, or the National Educational Technology Standards for Students and a currently corresponding visual art, theatre, music or dance process and anchor standard for the draft of the National Coalition of Core Arts Standards, set to be released in June of 2014 at the date of this publication. **It is important to note that these alignments may need to be revised once the official standards are released, depending on the changes made to the draft.**

Let's take STEAM out for a spin and see what our students can do once we get out of their way and become facilitators of learning rather than our current status quo. Our children are learning despite us, not because of us. It's time to disrupt that pattern and create a new prism of discovery. And it all starts with a Rainbow Room.

part 1 | the integration disruption

chapter 1 | what is S.T.E.A.M.?

Julia isn't smart. At least, she doesn't think so. Her brother, Henry, is a straight-A student. He always sits in the front of class and is the first to raise his hand when the teacher asks a question. All the teachers like Henry and at the parent/ teacher conferences, they all give him the highest praise imaginable. Henry knows how to play the school "game."

Julia, on the other hand, is relegated to the Rainbow Room. Literally. Her classroom is at the end of the hallway and her teacher has a big rainbow on the door. It's where they place all the kids who score poorly on their reading and math tests at the beginning of the school year. Nobody says this, of course, but Julia and all her classmates know it. Her teacher is pleasant enough, but there is a wearied measure in her tone as she reads from the Teacher's Guide about yet another grouping strategy for addition, as if she knows that she is just wasting her breath. But, she smiles anyway as she calls on various students to go to the interactive whiteboard and try some sample problems. Julia puts her head down, draws in her notebook and tries to look like she is working.

Every marking period, it's the same. She and Henry ride the bus home, carrying their report cards to their expectant parents. Henry's shouts "brilliant" and Julia's shouts "lack of meeting potential". Julia cries during the walks toward the house on these 4 days each year and Henry holds her hand and tells her that it will be alright. He tries to help his sister with her homework, but he can't understand what is so challenging about it. The answers to the questions are so plainly obvious! How can his sister not understand basic formulas and steps?

When they get home, their parents smile at Henry and tell him how proud they are of him. When they look at Julia's card, they tell her that they are proud of her too, for trying her best. It just makes her feel like even more of a failure. She didn't want to just try her best; she wanted to be her best. Her classes just don't make sense to her and it is so frustrating to sit in a room and never understand how all of the pieces fit together. It is all so fuzzy, as though the concepts are right within reach to her but still manage to slip through her tiny fingers.

As the school years continue, the gaps keep widening. Julia begins to not only dislike school - she resents it and everything it represents. She begins to retreat more into herself and pays less and less attention. Her teachers quietly assume that her trajectory is already set; there is nothing they can do. They don't give up on trying to teach Julia, but when she doesn't make progress, they all have an excuse as to why she isn't successful. And none of those excuses lie within their own teaching capacities.

By middle school, Julia and Henry are miles apart in their school pathways and each begin to think of themselves in a different way. Henry believes that he is capable of doing anything and that the world is his oyster. By comparison, Julia believes that she is capable of doing enough to get her through, after which she can have time to do the things she loves: drawing, sports, and being with her friends. She no longer thinks of herself as "dumb," but she's definitely no brainiac like Henry. That's his story, not hers.

Henry has a different issue. While he believes, without question, that the world is open to whatever he sets his mind to, he struggles to socially connect with his peers. He doesn't have very many friends and it is difficult for him to collaborate on projects and ideas. While his sister Julia has people that she can hang out with every day after school, Henry often opts to stay home and read a book or play a video game by himself. Henry cannot figure out how to build relationships with others because they always see him as the "know-it-all." But can he help it if he always has the right answers?

Stop. It's time for a disruption to this scenario. Both of these trajectories should sound familiar to you if you're an educator. It's a stereotype, yes, but there's a reason for the stereotype - because it's a reality. This kind of teaching and learning happens all the time: in every population, in every school. Even yours. Sure, maybe not this explicitly, but you certainly have students roaming your halls who can identify with this story and the divergent pathways it represents. Do you think your students could predict the outcome to this vignette for both Henry and Julia? You bet they could.

We need to change their story and its outcome. For far too long in education, this scene has been on repeat. Finally, we are at a point where it is not only possible, but imperative that we facilitate learning environments that are fluid, dynamic, and relevant. None of us go outside and look at a tree and say, "that's a tree, so that's science" or, "the sky is blue, so that's art." Our world is a beautiful, complex, and intricate tapestry of learning all in its own right. Why do we believe that we have the ability or the right to box it in behind brick walls and classroom doors in a place called school?

Integrating concepts, topics, standards and assessments is a powerful way to disrupt the typical course of events for our students and to help change this merry-go-round of "school." It takes what we do when we open the doors to the real world and places those same practices in our cycles of teaching and learning, thereby removing the brick walls and classroom doors. In the story of Henry and Julia, both have strengths and weaknesses with which the other can assist and leverage. By tapping into these areas and intentionally connecting through them, their stories can take a completely different turn.

Much of what we think could be disrupting education right now is, in truth, merely a misinterpretation. New standards are being implemented and this is causing many to believe that we have a huge turn in our educational system. Standards are just standards. They are simply a baseline benchmark for expectations of learning. The real driver of the change occurring is the foundation upon which these new standards rest. The standards being put into place call for process-based teaching and learning. We want to know not only *what* students know but *how* they know it and what they can *do* with it. No longer is it enough to just teach the content. Now we must also ensure that students can make that content personal to their own learning and use it to create new meaning for themselves. In order to accomplish this massive task, we must recognize that integration is the most efficient, effective, and authentic format for this kind of implementation.

Foundations of Integration

Integration as a concept can hold very different interpretations in both its definition and its implementation. This is a huge struggle, and possibly one of the reasons why integration isn't more prevalent in our schools today. Integration can easily be confused with enhancement. Often when consulting with educators I hear the, "oh, I'm already doing that" response when I ask if they are using arts integration in their classrooms. Then they proudly show me the shadow boxes they have created or the way they used "Fifty Nifty United States" to help their students memorize the names of all fifty states.

To be fair, there is nothing wrong with either of these examples. They are wonderful ways to enhance the curriculum. But it's not integration. Integration is the intentional act of finding, aligning, teaching and assessing two or more naturally-connected standards equitably with integrity to both content areas. To find out if you are truly integrating across content areas, ask yourself this question:

"What standards am I teaching and assessing?"

If you cannot identify both standards and explain how you are using and assessing both equitably in the lesson, then it is not an integrated approach. Think about our previous example of the shadow boxes - what standards are being taught and assessed with this activity? Additionally, it's not enough to just identify the standards after the lesson has been completed. For it to be an authentically integrated lesson, the standards must be identified intentionally during the lesson planning process. This way, the lesson is taught with both standards being addressed and assessed from the very beginning.

Integration is the intentional act of finding, aligning, teaching and assessing two or more naturally-connected standards equitably with integrity to both content areas.

Another example of integration-gone-wrong would be calling something a "STEM" lesson because you are having students use mobile devices or other technology during class. For instance, if you are working on a math lesson about fractions and are using a mobile app to have your students use flashcards for math facts, this is not a STEM lesson. Rather, you are using the technology to enhance or solidify knowledge and skills. To be a STEM lesson, the technology standards or processes would need to be identified during the planning process and then taught and applied in partnership with the math standards. This would then lead to an assessment of the skills and processes from both the math and technology standards as students work through the lesson.

Is this a more difficult task than simply making connections to other areas? Absolutely! There's no sugar-coating this: it takes more time to plan, collaborate, facilitate and assess authentically integrated lessons than if you were to simply add an arts or technology component to your traditional lesson plan or curriculum. However, the benefits to this kind of approach are astounding. Studies have shown that students who learn through authentically integrated lessons have better attendance, increased student stamina, and increased achievement in all populations - but particularly among special education and minority students. As an added bonus, when intentionally integrating across content areas, the ability to cover more content within a lesson or project is possible because of the broad skills and processes that are needed to be successful. So while integrated lessons seem to take more time, you are covering more ground in your curriculum than if you were to silo each standard individually.

Integration can occur in any content area and is not limited to one kind of approach. The ones we will focus on in this book are Arts Integration, STEM and STEAM. In particular, we will take a look at their similarities and differences, when it is appropriate to use each and how to begin moving through the integration process.

STEM, STEAM, and Everything In Between

The idea of STEM (Science, Technology, Engineering, and Mathematics) is not new one to most educators and anyone else who has been paying attention to education for the last 10 years or so. Currently, there are a multitude of STEM magnet programs, 1:1 device purchases for STEM initiatives in schools of every shape and size, and even a set of technology standards of practice that have been developed in many states and through the professional organization ISTE® (The International Society for Technology in Education). Yet, for all of the money that is being invested into the nuts and bolts of STEM, there is so much left to be done.

Implementation of STEM relies on more than equipment; it also requires a much deeper concentration on providing professional development which builds the capacity of teachers to understand and connect the content areas being addressed. We have seen this before in other attempts to integrate across content areas, most notably in Arts Integration initiatives. Too often, the struggle for schools in implementation of integrated models is that they invest in the *what* (strategies, tools, materials) rather that the *how* (professional development, curriculum design, collaborative planning). Teachers need more than just the tools required for integration across contents. They also need to know how to apply the tools to build a new opportunity for learning.

This is just one of several undeniable parallels between the STEM approach and Arts Integration. Both are grounded in process-based learning, require that the content areas are intentionally integrated in both standards and assessment, and use inquiry to drive instruction. Both are also commonly misunderstood and misinterpreted in their implementation. But is there a way and a need to utilize both approaches through a blended model of STEAM? Let's investigate STEM, Arts Integration and STEAM to discover what makes them unique and what qualities are shared in their approaches to integrated learning models.

STEM

STEM is the intentional connection between two or more of these selected content areas to drive instruction through observation, inquiry and problem solving as an approach to teaching and learning. Much has been proclaimed about the need for more STEM "programs" in our schools. The logic is simple: the wave of future economic prosperity lies in a workforce that is well-versed in rising job markets like science, technology, engineering and math. Thus, there has been an increased investment in STEM initiatives in schools. This includes, but is not limited to:

- providing mobile devices for students (sometimes in the forms of computer labs, and other times in the form of 1:1 – a single device for each student)

- after-school STEM clubs or programs

- STEM curriculum, where projects using STEM practices are embedded

- BYOD initiatives (bring your own device)

- STEM days to encourage hands-on exploration within each of these disciplines

- robotics programs

In reality, what we have been doing is investing in STEM enhancement. Providing students and teachers with access to technology is important, but it is not true STEM. Neither is having a set time and place to experiment with STEM practices. While we need to have this time and space as the first step in moving towards STEM, stopping here is doing STEM a disservice. To truly make an impact with STEM, we need our students to take what they know about these areas and connect them intentionally through lessons that are framed in inquiry, problem-solving, and creative applications.

STEM is the intentional connection between two or more of these selected content areas to drive instruction through observation, inquiry and problem solving.

Instead of STEM programs, we should be focused on STEM practices. Learning STEM-focused skills and processes in tandem with another content area is critical to ensure that they are not isolated, but rather a central partner to learning. STEM education provides a teaching and learning environment that not only teaches the skills in science, technology, engineering and mathematics, but also the means to connect these skills through the core processes of interpretation, communication, analysis and synthesis. This idea of STEM means that Science and Technology are being taught together, rather than as isolated areas of study. Or that Engineering and Math skills are being connected with integrity throughout a lesson and both areas are assessed on the final project. This makes the learning in all of these areas more meaningful and translates to better application in real life.

While the STEM initiative examples provided above are a wonderful start into the exploration of these four areas of study, the critical process of creativity and innovation is missing. Students in STEM programs may have more experiential learning opportunities, but they are limited to only science, technology, engineering and math. Our economy requires so much more than an understanding of these areas – it requires application, creation and ingenuity. STEM alone does not foster these essential nutrients.

Arts Integration

Arts integration is an approach to teaching and learning through which content is taught and assessed equitably in and through the arts. This provides students with the opportunity to explore multiple content areas simultaneously through the skills and processes learned in the arts classroom. Arts integration engages students in learning any content area in and through the arts. This means that any subject could be taught through the purposeful connection to a naturally-aligned arts standard. So students could be reading a Norman Rockwell painting while using Common Core ELA Standards and visual arts standards. Or students could explore the scientific method through the elements of music. As with STEM, this approach is not simply an "add-on," but the authentic connection of standards which are taught together and assessed equitably. Students are able to access skills, talents and processes learned in the arts classroom to explore other topics and develop a personal understanding of both content areas.

A beautiful element to Arts Integration which cannot be overlooked is it's capacity to unlock each student's unique access point of creativity and understanding of the world around them. Every child connects with the arts in some way - it is up to us to find it and use that as a way to foster their capacity for learning. And since Arts Integration is not constrained to only four areas, it can be used in any subject, provided that there is a naturally-aligned standard. There is enormous flexibility in this approach when used with integrity and purpose.

Arts Integration is an approach to teaching and learning through which content is taught and assessed equitably in and through the arts.

Arts integration also has some limitations in its approach - it is easily misinterpreted and can be difficult to move from enhancement to true integration. Too often, the arts are used as enhancement in the lesson (think of the "shadow boxes") rather than as a true means of connecting and communicating understanding. Additionally, it must be noted that arts specialists can feel threatened by arts integration as though the arts are being taught exclusively in the classroom and only for the purposes of accomplishing the other standards. **Arts integration can happen only if there is a strong arts program and dedicated art classes, since students need these skills and processes prior to engaging in an integrated lesson.** Yet without professional development, teachers can often miss this key element.

For the classroom teacher, Arts Integration sometimes seems intimidating as an approach. This is because teachers are nervous about their own artistic abilities, and also their ability to effectively facilitate a lesson that includes authentic arts standards. Yet Arts Integration strategies have a variety of levels, and many can be implemented quite quickly in classrooms as we will discover in Chapter 3.

STEAM

STEAM is a way to take the benefits of STEM and complete the package by integrating these principles in and through the arts. STEAM is an educational approach to learning that uses Science, Technology, Engineering, the Arts and Mathematics as access points for guiding student inquiry, dialogue and critical thinking. STEAM takes STEM to the next level: it allows students to connect their learning in these critical areas together with arts practices, elements, design principles, and standards to provide the whole pallet of learning at their disposal. STEAM removes limitations and replaces them with wonder, critique, inquiry, and innovation.

STEAM brings together the critical components of how and what, and laces them together with why. Think of STEAM as teaching through integrated network hubs where information is curated, shared, explored and molded into new ways of seeing and being through collaborative risk taking and creativity. This means that students are using the skills and processes learned in science, technology, engineering, the arts and mathematics to think deeply, ask non-Googleable questions and solve problems.

STEAM is an educational approach to learning that uses Science, Technology, Engineering, the Arts and Mathematics as access points for guiding student inquiry, dialogue and critical thinking.

The pathway to STEAM is exciting, but can also be dangerous without an understanding of what STEAM truly means in both its intention and its implementation. Like its STEM predecessor, STEAM can stop short of its best manifestation without several core components:

- **STEAM is an integrated approach to learning** which requires an intentional connection between standards, assessments and lesson design/ implementation

- True STEAM experiences involve two or more standards from Science, Technology, Engineering, Math and the Arts to be **taught AND assessed in and through each other**

- **Inquiry, collaboration, and an emphasis on process-based learning** are at the heart of the STEAM approach

- **Utilizing and leveraging the integrity of the arts** themselves is essential to an authentic STEAM initiative

In order to accomplish these goals, schools must consider a variety of factors, such as:

- Collaborative planning, including a cross-section of teachers on each team
- Adjusting scheduling to accommodate a new way of teaching and learning
- Professional development for all staff in STEAM practices and principles
- STEAM schema-mapping for the curriculum and assessment design process
- Alignment and unpacking of standards and assessments
- Seamless lesson implementation processes and strategies

This approach to learning is certainly not an easy task, but the benefits to students and the entire school community are tremendous. Students and teachers engaged in STEAM make more real-life connections so that school is not a place where you go to learn but instead becomes the entire experience of learning itself. We are always learning, always growing, always experimenting. **School doesn't have to be a place, but rather a frame of mind that uses the Arts as a lever to explosive growth, social-emotional connections, and the foundation for the innovators of our future.**

There are also some key differences between STEAM and Arts Integration. STEAM truly focuses on how the arts intersect and interact within and through Science, Technology, Engineering and Mathematics. While other areas can also play in the STEAM sandbox, such as reading informational science texts, they may be used more for an enhancement or subsidiary role rather than truly integrated. Arts Integration, on the other hand, can be used more broadly in any area which contains a naturally-aligned standard with the selected arts standard. Arts Integration also typically focuses more attention on the process and end-product, whereas STEAM sets out with the core intent to solve a problem.

Currently, much of the conversation around STEAM has been focused on artistic design principles. While this is certainly one approach to STEAM, it is a rather limited view of how the arts can connect, support, and deepen STEM areas. Arts Integration is a close relative to STEAM and as such, the same practices and elements from all of the arts areas that are used within Arts Integration may also be applied to STEAM given the appropriate standard alignment. For instance, the music elements of pitch, duration, and form could all connect with a variety of STEM concepts. The same is true for the dance elements of Energy, Space and Time. Be careful not to limit your scope of STEAM to just include visual arts and design when the whole spectrum of the Arts are at your disposal.

How to STEAM

Now that we have the foundations of what STEAM is and why it's important, the next step is to understand how to implement STEAM with integrity. Many schools claim to be "STEAM Schools," and yet their model of instructional implementation is weak or simply brushes the surface of what STEAM truly requires. Instead, STEAM has a foundation of integration at it's core, which means that each curricular area should be both taught in its own right, as well as connected through standards and assessments when used in tandem.

What is outlined below is a process of lesson planning that is authentic to successful integration models and which honors the core intent of areas addressed through STEAM. This is one of the most important pieces of the entire book, as it provides you with a blueprint for implementation that is genuine to the practices of STEAM and simultaneously maintains the integrity of both the STEM and Arts content. Think of this process as a cycle which is grounded in integration and through which meaningful teaching and learning takes place. We will explore this in much more detail in Chapter 8, but for now, this provides you with a basic framework.

STEAM Process Cycle

1. Investigate: Collaborative

Begin by collaborating with students to define a topic of interest. It is critical that we empower and involve our students in their learning and the investigation stage provides us with this opportunity right from the start. In this stage of STEAM, teachers and students explore a broad range of topics, ideas or problems in a particular content area of focus. For instance, you may begin by focusing on the Great Depression, processes that artists use, or security concerns at large sporting events. All of these are "Big Buckets" that have many different avenues for learning exploration. Think widely in this portion of the process, with the understanding that you will narrow into a specific piece of the topic later on. Encourage discussions and facilitate these as collaborative learning conversations to select your topic of focus. As you choose your topic and begin to move into the discovery phase, think about an essential question you would like to answer as a group.

Note: this is often the most difficult stage for TEACHERS but the most exciting stage for students. This requires that teachers relinquish control of their classroom and lesson planning to their students. Teachers become facilitators of learning which guide the conversations but never dictate what topic will be covered. If this is too much risk to start, teachers may narrow the choices of topics based upon their students' current location on the curriculum continuum for their class.

2. **Discover: Teacher-led**

During the discovery phase, you'll create a curriculum schema map about the chosen topic, idea or problem. To do this, start by placing the chosen broad focus in the center of a piece of paper and surrounding it with everything that may influence, cause, or result from that particular topic. You'll begin to see trends, patterns, or areas you would like to explore more deeply. Try it using the beginning schema map below for the Scientific Method. Explore how each of these areas and subtopics might relate to the Scientific Method.

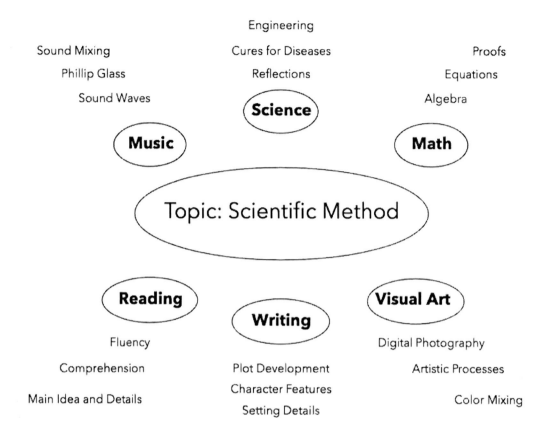

As you notice these areas, draw lines attaching them to each other. This provides you with an easily recognizable pathway for searching and selecting naturally-aligned standards. Try to be as thorough as possible - you never know where a connection will appear. Look at the example on the next page and some of the lines that have been started. Do you see any other connections? What other lines would you draw?

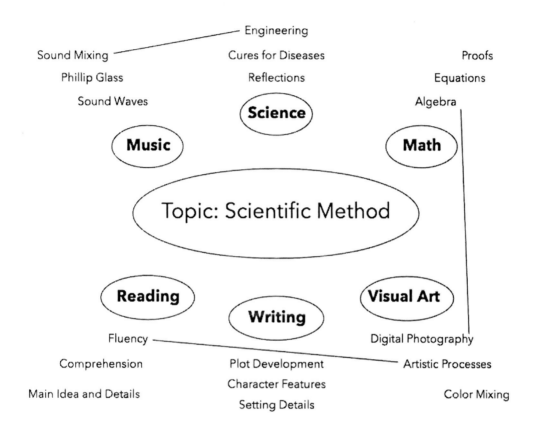

3. Connect: Teacher-led

Once you have created your curricular schema map, choose one or two connected areas to your broad topic. For instance, if my topic was the the Scientific Method,

I may choose engineering and sound mixing as two areas that I would like to connect and explore in relationship to each other based upon an essential question. The essential question might be "How do we create sound?" and we could explore that question from either or both of those two areas. From there, a curriculum map can be created that aligns two naturally-connected standards in both content areas (science and music), as well as an equitable assessment for both standards being addressed.

This curriculum map can take many different formats. You may have mapping software for your school or district that you use, or you may have never created a map before. How you create the map isn't as important as the key components that you place in your curriculum map. Here is an example of a simple curriculum map design that will help you to design an authentic integrated lesson:

Topic	Content Standard	Arts Standard	Assessments	Lesson Idea
Scientific Method	**Engineering HS-ETS1-4.** Use a computer simulation to model the impact of proposed solutions to a complex real-world problem with numerous criteria and constraints on interactions within and between systems relevant to the problem.	**MU:Cr1-T.II.a** Explore sounds and compose or improvise multiple musical ideas, excerpts, melodies or arrangements that exhibit originality, unity and variety for a specific purpose or to express intent, personal interests or experiences with digital tools and resources.	Student will listen to each group perform both the live and edited versions of their song poems. Each student will complete a rubric analysis of how each group used mixing and mastering to enhance the poem.	Explore how engineers mix music in a sound studio using the scientific method.

You can view this map come to life in the lesson Producing Beats in part 3 of this resource. If you're looking for a curriculum map template to use in conjunction with your own schema maps, you can find one below.

STEAM Curriculum Map

Topic	Content Standard	Arts Standard	Assessments	Lesson Idea

4. Create: Teacher-led, followed by Collaborative

Once your standards and assessments are aligned between your chosen content areas, a lesson can now be developed to guide students in their learning about the broader topic through the two chosen standards. This process should be inquiry driven, where students are presented with a problem or question in which they will need to learn and use content knowledge to influence the context of the situation.

You can develop this lesson using your essential question from the Discovery phase and the curriculum map from the Connect phase. Begin by placing your essential question at the top of the page. Next, write your standards from the curriculum map side-by-side. This is important as it sets up an equitable weight for each standard right from the beginning. If you place one standard on top of the other, inadvertently you will perceive the top standard as more important.

Once you have your standards written side-by-side, develop your assessment using the idea you crafted in your curriculum map. Your assessment should be at the same level of cognitive demand as your standard. So, if the standard is asking students to analyze a problem, the assessment should also be asking students to analyze. This creates a more tightly aligned, authentic learning experience which is measuring what the standard requires.

Once these pieces are set into place, choose a real-world issue or application that could be used to highlight the chosen topic and standards. For instance, in the case of our selected Scientific Method topic, you may use the advances in studio engineering and producing to reflect a more genuine listening experience rather than a more polished "airbrushed" sound. From there, use your standards and assessment to guide the instruction around the topic in order to better understand and create solutions to the issue or application you have chosen. In addition to the standards, essential question, and assessment, be sure to include the following components in your lesson plan:

- Big Idea (your topic and it's application, perhaps)

- Materials of Instruction

- Vertical alignment (what is happening before and after this lesson to put this piece into context)

- Pre-engagement, transitions, and focal lesson steps

- Key vocabulary for both content areas

 Sample lessons are included in part three of this book, as well as a sample lesson template that you may use to help you move through this planning process.

5. Reflect: Collaborative

Once students have moved through the lesson and completed their project or assignment, they must be able to have time to reflect and critique their own work, as well as that of their peers. This can be done through self-assessments, rubrics, portfolios, artists' statements, or peer reviews. Similarly, teachers and administrators must also have time to engage in the reflection process based upon the results of the lesson process and products.

Also included in part three of this book are sample peer review sheets and teacher reflection prompts. It is critical that students be involved in the reflection process for both their own work and of the lesson itself so that they may develop an understanding of their own strengths and weaknesses, and learning style preferences. This provides students with an opportunity to own their growth development and invest in the learning process.

In this same vein, educators must take the time to reflect upon their own teaching practice. How much information did you give to the students rather than guide with student input? What kind of questions did you ask? What was a triumph of this lesson and what was a struggle? By asking these kinds of reflective prompts, we activate and integrate our own learning through our teaching, thereby continuing the cycle. This reflection process then serves as a platform for the next STEAM lesson through investigating the gaps and areas of interest that both parties (teacher and student) identify.

Chapter Review

STEAM is much more than an exciting classroom project or including technology and art into science, engineering and math content areas. It is a rich, highly-developed approach to learning which endeavors to provide students with opportunities to explore, discover and create new possibilities through their learning experiences.

In this chapter we have covered an overview of integration and how this manifests itself authentically in STEM, Arts Integration and STEAM lessons within the classroom. As we move into our next chapter, we'll begin to explore what this looks like in practice, along with a variety of examples of how individual schools and districts approach the process to best meet their evolving needs. Before moving on, take a moment to review the major concepts in this chapter and reflect upon their impact for your unique application with the following questions:

1. What are your concerns and celebrations with the integration process?

2. When do you think it is appropriate to use STEM, Arts Integration and STEAM? Do you have a personal preference?

3. What do you see as a critical component for success in your classroom, school or district? How do you plan to ensure this piece is in place?

4. What discoveries have you made about yourself or your own teaching practice thus far in this process?

chapter 2 | what to do after the grant is over
case study #1

This is the first of three case studies that will appear in this book. Each case study provides a practical view of how different schools approach STEAM differently. Please keep this in mind as you work through these examples. While these are intended to share with you some models of the STEAM approach, they are not molds. Each school has a unique culture and community and what works for one may not work for yours. Yet we can learn so much through the experiences of others, both in their triumphs and in their struggles, which is why the time has been taken to include these examples in this book. I sincerely thank each of these schools for graciously sharing with all of us their journeys and am so proud to be able to provide a spotlight on their endeavors.

Piney Grove Elementary School

Location: Kernersville, North Carolina

Profile:
- 632 students in grades K-5
- 31% receive Free and Reduced Meals
- Average class size is 23 students
- Daily Attendance Rate of 96%
- Student demographics include 83% Caucasian, 7% Black, 6% Hispanic, 2% Two or more races, and 1% Asian
- Community: Suburban

STEAM Initiative Leaders:
Susan Frye (Principal), Natalie Strange (Media Coordinator), Melissa Edwards (Technology Integration Specialist)

Timeframe:
This is a new initiative for the 2013-2014 school year.

What happens when the grant runs out? Many schools face this issue after using the grant to purchase resources, tools and professional development and Piney Grove was no different. They had received a grant to purchase technology supports for their building, but by 2013, the grant period was over and the money had been exhausted. What they had left over were a few Kindle Fire tablets and a room being used for storage.

So what do you do next? How do you build in sustainability and support for technology integration if the devices have been your area of focus? The school knew it needed to make a shift into creating an environment where the use of the devices became a hub for exploring the opportunities those devices presented. And, they needed to do it at little or no cost. Their community was a middle-grounder: not enough money was available to purchase extra resources and devices, but their average median income didn't qualify them for additional funding supports. The school needed to find a way to utilize what they had to provide an interactive, creative, and engaging learning environment that embraced and integrated the technology they already had at their disposal.

The Power of a Challenge

Creative solutions most often happen when limited options are presented. Such was the case when Natalie Strange and Melissa Edwards began brainstorming around what could be done with these extra Kindle Fires. Natalie, the media coordinator, didn't want to see these extra devices going to waste or simply being used as a substitute for another device in class. She wanted to break the mold and come up with a totally different way to make sure that a few tablets could feed the instructional needs of hundreds of students.

Natalie is used to breaking the mold. On any given day, there may be parent volunteers supporting instruction in the media center or working on construction of a new reading area for students. She has had a castle built to house all of the fairytale books in her library, has set up areas to explore 39 Clues where you can concoct your own edible drink based on the clues that you find, and has even employed a "shelf elf" to appear through magical doors on the bookshelves to help books come to life for students. She coordinates whole-school support systems across curricular areas, and works hard to ensure that the magic of stories are brought to life in her teaching space. Her philosophy is that the more that students are excited by something, the more likely they are to pursue it. So when it came to creating a learning experience that embraced not only technology devices but also the worlds that technology could open for students, she was determined to develop something that supported the idea of discovery. So she turned to her district resource for instructional technology integration, Melissa Edwards, for some collaboration and guidance.

Melissa is an instructional technologist for Winston-Salem/Forsyth County Schools and also a former 4th grade classroom teacher. She is a passionate advocate for technology and the arts, and utilizes technology as a platform for integration, rather than as a destination of integration. Piney Grove is one of the schools she continually supports as a resource and when she visited with Natalie Strange, she knew based upon their conversation that they were on the verge of something special. They began by thinking about ways that they could use the Kindle Fires for instruction in small groups. It would be hard to do it during student time in the media center, and that's when they began thinking about housing the Kindle Fires in a different space. They discovered a small room that was only being used for storage and when they went in, Melissa saw several old globes that still had the old Soviet Union boundaries labeled. This became their light bulb moment, because after all - who was going to use globes that were no longer relevant?

Melissa and Natalie began asking "what if" questions. What if students could paint the globes with chalkboard paint and use them to draw the path of a jet stream or outline a trench in the ocean? What if the Kindles were used as a station for exploration through apps, but there were other stations with laptops and hands-on activities? What if this was designed to enhance and deepen instruction in any area that a teacher chose, and was a totally flexible and open space? Through these questions, the Piney Grove STEAM Lab was born.

Creating Buy-In

Once the two women had a basic outline of what this new STEAM Lab could look like and its possibilities for learning, they immediately took it to the school's principal, Susan Frye. Susan is a strong supporter of teacher leadership and student inquiry and believes in allowing new approaches to be explored without fear of failure.

When approached by Natalie and Melissa, Susan expressed her belief as a leader in supporting people to share their gifts when it comes to trying out new ideas for instruction. Because of this, she not only gave Natalie and Melissa permission to give their idea a try, she became a staunch supporter of the initiative right from the start. After working through the possibilities of the STEAM Lab, and collaborating with Natalie and Melissa on what would be needed logistically to get the Lab up and running, Susan presented the concept during a staff meeting early on in the process. She shared the vision for the Lab and asked for teacher input as a valuable part of bringing this idea to life. She then turned the floor over the Natalie and Melissa, who provided some sample ideas of how teachers could use the Lab, based upon curricular topics that they knew would be coming up soon in several grade levels.

From there, Susan, Natalie and Melissa sent out a teacher survey in regards to developing the STEAM Lab as a space that would be utilized for integrated learning. This survey asked teachers to identify their needs, how they could see using the Lab, and what scheduling options they would prefer. The team then took this feedback and created a sample lesson thread that could be explored with the stations in the STEAM Lab. They cleaned out the room and set it up as a new Lab space and then invited teachers in to try out the Lab using the sample lesson thread. This hands-on experience, along with the teacher survey, provided a great deal of teacher buy-in to using the Lab and exploring its possibilities with their students. As teachers moved through each of the stations, they began brainstorming with their colleagues how they could use these stations for instruction and how to bring a topic to life through the use of the Lab.

The STEAM Lab Brought to Life

The logistics of the STEAM Lab are some of what sets it apart and offers incredible opportunities for students and teachers alike. Here are a few key elements of this school's approach:

Scheduling

The STEAM Lab is open on a flexible schedule that is completely driven by teacher and student needs. There is currently a parent volunteer in the Lab 2-3 days a week who acts as the Lab facilitator. A sign-up sheet for the Lab is posted and teachers sign up for a time whenever they need it. Depending on the size of the topic focus, a teacher may sign up for use of the Lab 3 days a week or maybe only twice a month. Each Lab rotation is for a 45-60 minute block to allow students enough time to explore each station. Additionally, teachers sign up for the Lab in place of another content block during the day. This means that they may come to the Lab during their Language Arts, Math, Science or Social Studies block and use the Lab as the space for instruction during that day. Thus, the STEAM Lab does not become an extra add-on to the day, but is used instead as a location for an integrated lesson used within the traditional curriculum.

Teacher Roles

The teacher involvement and roles in the STEAM Lab thus far have been variable. Teachers have the ability to stay in the room and to help move students through the stations and ask guiding questions along the way. Many have taken this opportunity to formatively assess student learning through the centers, gathering feedback on student preferences and learning styles as well as comprehension and application of the chosen topic. Some teachers choose to allow the Lab's facilitator to guide their students through the stations while they use the time to provide more individualized instruction to students who may need more support, or to pull-out students for things like DIBELS testing which is difficult to do during traditional classroom time.

Teachers also take on varying roles in the planning and development process. Many are just beginning to learn and understand the integration process and can be intimidated by the approach. The STEAM Lab provides them with a safe alternative to a fully integrated lesson that they are facilitating on their own. Teachers collaborate with Natalie on ideas and standards for upcoming units and projects, and Natalie supports them by finding resources to support the topic of exploration in the lab. Natalie compiles the resources through the use of organizational technology tools like Symbaloo (www.symbaloo.com) and LiveBinders (www.livebinders.com) which can then be accessed via the devices in the Lab or by teachers should they choose to include them in their traditional classroom settings. Some teachers are more involved than others in the process of developing the integrated experience in the lab, but all take a hands-on role in collaborating through the process based upon current units of study.

Here is an example of a Symbaloo that was developed to house web resources for circuits and electricity study in 3rd grade:

Stations

There are currently four stations available to students in the lab. Each station has a variety of options for choice-based ways to explore, discover, apply and create around the centralized topic being studied that day. These stations include:

The Wonder Station. This is an area where several laptops with headphones are available to students to explore the topic through Wonderopolis (www.wonderopolis.com).

The Vocabulary Station. This is an area of the lab that has a magnetic chalkboard with a set of vocabulary words. These words can be mixed and matched with their definitions and extensions to allow for tactile word-play which is important to the chosen focus.

The Kindle Fire Station. This is where students can use the Symbaloo file of apps and websites to explore the content in more depth and to discover multiple ways in which the concept can be manifested.

The Creation Station. This is an area of the Lab where students are given a task or project to complete about the topic. They can use what they have learned at other stations to support their creative output, or they can create first and then discover and explore other options that have been developed through the other stations and resources.

Opportunities and Obstacles

In creating a unique approach like this to STEAM, there are always learning experiences that provide great opportunities and others that present some realistic obstacles along the way. This STEAM Lab has not been embraced by the entire faculty. Some teachers simply do not use it at all, even though others have truly jumped on board and are realizing its outstanding potential. The leaders of this initiative believe this may be due to the fact that it's a new and relatively untested model of instruction within the school. Having an administrator like Susan who recognizes this, and is willing to patiently yet strategically move this initiative forward despite the hiccups is essential. Anytime that a new approach is presented, you will always face some push back until the method has been proven successful and teachers have been given time to explore the idea themselves and get comfortable with the approach. This obstacle provides an opportunity for an organic approach to STEAM to take root. As teachers discover how engaged their students are in learning while in the STEAM lab, they will continue to take advantage of the resource and encourage their colleagues to take part. Some of the most powerful initiatives are centered around teachers who are modeling for their colleagues and validating the experience.

Another clear obstacle lies in the fact that the media coordinator is doing a bulk of the planning, resource collection and securing facilitation for the Lab. This is most likely not sustainable. After all, what would happen to the Lab if Natalie were to leave? More professional development in integrated lesson design and an intentional integrated collaborative planning time would be helpful in empowering classroom teachers to build and facilitate their own lessons. This takes time and given that this is the first year of the concept, a tremendous amount of experience in the power of integrated learning has already been provided with the hands-on structure of the Lab environment. As teachers engage in more professional development on integrated learning, the opportunities for STEAM to be used throughout the building and within the classrooms abound. Rather than STEAM being a location where students go, the approach will become the way students learn in all areas of the school.

Finally, not all schools have a spare room or a space to set up a STEAM Lab environment. At first glance, this could be a stumbling block if you are trying to replicate this exact model. However, there are many other options that could be explored. There could be a STEAM storage closet that houses the materials that would be needed. This way, teachers could create the STEAM Labs in their own classrooms. Another option would be to have a STEAM Lab cart that can float between classrooms and be pulled into instruction. This yields the opportunity for even more spontaneous STEAM explorations without the confines of a sign-up sheet when the Lab is open. As Melissa Edwards stated, "This isn't going to look the same everywhere, and it shouldn't" in order to be successful. The idea is that this is a flexible, hands-on approach that can be designed to fit the unique needs and strengths of your own school.

Conclusion

The conclusion of a grant can be an obstacle, or it can present an opportunity for a new way to sustain what has already been developed. By viewing their lack of funding support as an opportunity, Piney Grove spring-boarded their previous success into a whole new way to empower students in their own learning. Additionally, because of their careful implementation, a supportive administrator, a collaborative approach with teachers, and tremendous flexibility, the STEAM Lab has the potential to continue to grow and provide an environment where innovation is valued and expected. Life after a grant certainly looks bright for this North Carolina school.

chapter 3 | arts-integrated s.t.e.a.m. strategies

We have a lot of art that decorates the walls in our home. Some of those pieces are photographs of our family and some are paintings and prints that we have collected over time. A few are vinyl letterings that have meaningful phrases to us. One of these vinyl letterings that is located on the stairway down to our finished basement reads, "Hands can build a house, but only hearts can build a home" and it reminds us why we worked so hard to finish our basement ourselves.

We spent many weeknights, weekends, and holidays shopping at our local home improvement store, studding up the walls, adding plumbing and electrical, finishing drywall, painting and selecting finishes. It took us the better part of a year and quite a bit of our savings invested into that project, and we did almost 90% of it by ourselves. Yes, it saved us money, but that wasn't the reason we chose to do it ourselves. We wanted to know that what we created truly reflected who we are as a family, what our needs were, and that we did it together. We put our hearts into that project and now it is a sanctuary for the many facets of our daily life.

What is a Strategy?

As we move into this next chapter of strategies, I want you to keep this do-it-yourself motivation in mind. The strategies are the hands that help you to stud up the walls of your lesson. They act in service of the standards you choose to align. But the heart of your teaching lies in what you do with those strategies and how you use them intentionally within your lessons and assessments. Strategies are the conduit to a full-bodied STEAM lesson. Don't get so caught up in the collection of great tools that you stop at merely framing your lesson through the use these strategies. Challenge yourself to learn these strategies with the purpose of embedding them authentically through a STEAM lesson to truly realize their maximum benefit.

This chapter will provide you with indispensable arts-integrated strategies which can be used within a STEAM lesson to deepen the learning and move students smoothly through the arts and content standards simultaneously. Each strategy provided includes step-by-step instructions for implementation and lists a corresponding lesson plan and assessment, which can be found in part 3 of this book. This way, you are able to see the strategy in isolation, and then immediately reference what it looks like in practice through a lesson. Additionally, you will find strategies highlighting each Arts area to showcase that STEAM can happen through not only visual art and design, but also music, theatre and movement.

Strategies are the conduit to a full-bodied STEAM lesson.

Key Elements of an Integration Strategy

When reviewing integration strategies to use outside of and within a STEAM lesson, be sure to look for the following key elements:

•A deep connection to an arts standard, process or skill.

•The use for the strategy is clearly evident.

•The strategy unfolds sequentially leading to higher cognitive demands

•The "doing" is placed within the students' hands, not the teacher's.

Let's take a look at these elements in a bit more detail. In the first element, it's important to ensure that the strategy you are considering is truly built upon a specific arts standard, process or skill. This means that the strategy is either using or breaking down a specific standard or element from the arts area into a process for new learning. There could be multiple standards addressed within a single strategy, and most likely only one or two broad skills or elements. Be sure to take the time to understand what your chosen strategy is addressing so that when you embed it into a lesson, you are doing so with integrity to the standards you have chosen to align.

Make sure that the use for the strategy in both the arts and the STEM content area is evident to both you and your students. You should be able to review the strategy and see how both content areas are being explored in the activity or process being defined. If not, the strategy may be a better fit for a non-integrated lesson or concept.

As you move through the strategy, consider how each step is leading to a deeper level of cognitive demand. Strategies that are one-note and horizontal don't achieve the same level of vigorous critical thinking and problem-solving that strategically sequential strategies offer. Look for strategies that start off at a relatively easy cognitive level (recall, observe or define) and through each step adds a new level of cognitive demand (analysis, synthesis, evaluation and creation). This moves your students through the process in a non-threatening and organic capacity.

Finally, observe how much of the work is being done by the students throughout the use of the strategy. If the students are passive participants or simply following directions, then the strategy is more focused on your delivery as the teacher. Instead, high leverage integration strategies place experiential learning opportunities in front of the students with teachers taking a more facilitative role. This makes the whole learning process more hands-on for students and is authentic to the core purpose of a STEAM approach.

Using Strategies Effectively

Integrated arts strategies are a critical component to any STEAM lesson, assessment and culture. They act as the levers for meaningful STEAM learning. But in order for the strategies to be used most effectively, there are a few foundational principles that need to be followed. First, use the strategy as a means to an end, rather than the end itself. Second, teach the strategy in isolation and then weave it into the lesson. Finally, focus on the big picture and not on the individual time spent on the strategy.

Integration strategies are simply that: strategies. They are not a lesson, nor are they meant to be used as merely a fun break in the middle of the day. Rather, strategies are designed as a pathway towards learning for the purpose of deeply connecting two content areas. This means that the strategy should be used in service of the lesson, not as the lesson itself. With this in mind, think through how you plan to leverage the strategy as a conduit for student learning during a STEAM lesson. Simultaneously, recognize the importance of the strategy and give it the dedicated time it deserves.

Strategies require that classroom time is dedicated to only working through the strategy in isolation from a lesson if they are to be used successfully. This means that you will need to plan on working through just the strategy, which could take 30-45 minutes, before weaving it in through an integrated lesson. This typically causes a lot of stress and worry when I introduce this foundational piece. After all, who has 30-45 minutes to dedicate to anything that isn't a core lesson plan? You do. Here's why: when you introduce the strategy in isolation during classroom time, you are setting your lesson up for maximum levels of student achievement.

First, by introducing the strategy in the classroom, students are prepared to consider your classroom a laboratory of learning, rather than a pulpit of information. You are setting them up for an inquiry-based learning experience which will take place in your classroom. If you plan to teach a STEAM lesson in your classroom, then it only makes sense that the strategy which serves that lesson also be introduced in that same classroom. Plus, the skills students need to successfully move through that strategy will be taught specifically in the arts classroom. You need for them to have those skills ahead of the strategy so that they spend time on the application of, rather than the acquisition of, those skills. Secondly, by spending the time isolating the strategy ahead of the lesson, you can move through that strategy and its corresponding understandings much faster during the lesson itself. Students will be able to more deeply connect the tissues of learning comprehension with their background knowledge and experiences of the strategy. This will lead to a strengthened foundation through which you can springboard the creative and critical-thinking process.

With all of this in mind, don't focus on the time you spend on strategies vs. lesson and assessment. Instead, think of them as a complete package and bundle your time to move through the pieces in a more cohesive format. Not every integrated lesson needs to be a unit or project! In fact, many if not most STEAM lessons can be accomplished in 2-3 class periods depending upon the content being addressed. Keep in mind, too, that when moving through an integrated lesson, you are providing a way for students to learn the information deeply and in connection with another area. This means that you will be spending less time reviewing and repeating concepts because students will have learned them comprehensively the first time it was taught. So don't watch the clock! Instead, think about your time broadly and trust that by moving through this process authentically, your students will not only achieve - they will thrive.

Strategy Cards

Each arts area will be given its own dedicated section and include 3-4 strategies which can be utilized for STEAM concepts and lessons. The strategies will be formatted so that you are aware of the arts area they address, suggestions for its use, a corresponding lesson and assessment page for an example of how it can be used in a lesson, and step-by-step directions for implementation.

VISUAL ARTS

The strategies outlined in this section include pieces in observation and in creating. Choose to use what is comfortable for you and then as you experience success, try to step a bit outside of your comfort zone.

iNOTICE[3]

Visual Art Focus: Analysis   **STEM Focus**: Deep observation and to prompt attention to fine detail

Lesson and Assessment Reference in Part 3: Finger "Prints" (Grades 3-5)

Sequence:

This is a flexible strategy for extending and deepening learning of any STEM concept through the arts. This technique is easily accessible for all teachers and students because it doesn't require knowledge within the arts itself, yet it is something that all artists inherently do throughout their work. What's more, it's also something that scientists and mathematicians do as they hone their skills and work to solve a problem.

1. **Choose a composition.** This could be a piece of artwork, music, choreographed dance, or theater performance. The type of art chosen doesn't matter - just that you choose something with some depth or nuance that forces intent observation.

2. **Ask students to view or listen to the whole composition.** Have students look at the whole piece or listen to the whole song. This gives them time to take it all in and get some context for what comes next.

3. **Choose something to notice.** Here's where it gets fun! Explain that you will be calling on a student who has something about the piece that they would like to point out to the group - something that they notice. Also explain that whatever that item is, you will be calling on two more people to notice something different about that same item.

4. **Begin the observations.** Ask a student who is ready to tell the class something that they notice or observe. When they point it out, ask another person in the class what else they notice about that object or element, followed by one more student. They may not state the same observation, but may ask questions about that item that are not clear to them, state something that it reminds them of, or go into more detail about the item or element in their description.

5. **Continue the strategy.** Repeat this strategy until everyone has gotten a turn in the class. Feel free to stop during their observations and discuss anything interesting or explore something they notice in more depth.

Essential Question: How can we express our learning through observation?

Badge Craft

Visual Art Focus: All Visual Art Elements   **STEM Focus**: Using concepts from the popular game, "Minecraft", students are provided opportunities to close read for evidence investigation.

Lesson and Assessment Reference in Part 3: Stained Glass Shapes (Grades K-2)

Sequence:
This strategy brings in concepts from gaming to define and express their analysis and synthesis of a specific topic, idea or problem. First, the use of a badge provides both an assessment and a learning tool. Badges are small awards that are received when a level is completed or a skill is mastered in a game. In this example, the badge is being used to both collect the synthesized understanding of the information and as a final product which represents mastery of the skills needed to produce that understanding.

1. **Give all students a blank badge template** with a topic you would like to address written in the center (ie: scientific method, reasoning, operations, etc).

2. **Share each visual arts element as a station with students.** For instance, there is a line station, a color station, a shape station, etc. Explore each element in detail by asking students to show each of these elements in some way as a class.

3. **At each station, place a key piece of information about the selected topic** that students will need to read closely.

4. **In groups, students will go to each station, read the information, and then create a representation of that information using only the visual art element found** at that station. All members of the group will need to collaborate to create the one representation using the element. Students will then transfer their representation onto their badge template.

5. **Rotate groups to each station** until their badges are filled with a representation about the topic using each visual art element.

Essential Question: How does collaboration effect investigation?

Whose Line is it Anyway?

Visual Art Focus: Line   **STEM Focus**: Geometry

Lesson and Assessment Reference in Part 3: Font Marketing (Grades 9-12)

Sequence:
This is a straightforward strategy that is focused intensely on lines and their use in geometrical concepts. By forcing the collaboration between partners in a final word that represents the topic or item chosen, students need to rethink the creation process to incorporate both ideas equitably and in a way that enhances the work as

a whole, rather than creating something that is jamming together two distinctly different ideas.

1. **Pick a topic you'd like students to investigate a**nd collaborate upon (ie: functions, patterns, inference, summary, etc) and share that term with the class.

2. **Ask students to observe how the word is written with lines.** Are they short, long, straight, curvy, angled, etc? Have an open discussion about how the letters are shaped in the word and if it captures the meaning of the word itself.

3. **Have students write down the word at the top of a blank piece of paper.** Then, ask them to think about and investigate with a partner what that word means. Write their definition underneath the original word.

4. **Each student should then try to write the word again, but only use lines that would reflect the meaning of the word.** (ie: collaborate would have lines that were closer together, possibly curvy, and may all be the same height and width).

5. **Students share their re-lined words** with their partner and discuss their line choice.

6. **Finally, have students create a collaborative word drawing with their partner.** Using the same word, one student begins to draw the word using their line choice and at a point when the partner is ready, they take over the drawing of the word with their line choice.

Essential Question: In what ways can we express our understanding of a concept?

6 Dots of Separation

Visual Art Focus: Stippling technique/patterns   **STEM Focus**: Moving an idea from an abstract concept to a realistic manifestation

Lesson and Assessment Reference in Part 3: Proportionate People (Grades 6-8)

Sequence:

In this strategy, students are constantly considering how a smaller segment is part of the whole idea. This is an important concept in all of the STEAM areas and combining the stippling technique with grids is helpful to make this idea more concrete. The final section of reimagining the original composition by changing the order of the original grid is critical to the tinkering process that is at the heart of STEAM. To ensure success, keep the paper size consistent and use the same amount of gridlines as there are number of students in the class. 6"x6" paper is recommended for a high quality final product if not using the digital option provided below.

1. **Observe several examples of artwork using the Stippling process** and have students reflect upon what they see. Ask questions such as how the artist may have accomplished the effect, what tools they envision might be needed, and how spacing of the dots changes the overall effect. **Stippling is a visual art technique that uses a combination of dots to create a picture.**

2. **Provide each student with a clean piece of white paper** and a variety of markers in different colors and tip sizes.

3. **Overlay a grid on top of a piece of geometric art** from artists such as Kandinsky and Bruce Bodden as an overhead projection. Ask students to notice the shapes within each grid area.

4. **Each student can select one box of the grid** to recreate using the stippling technique.

5. **Students fill their entire paper with their grid-box selection** using the stippling technique. Their dots should combine to create the shape or pattern from the original grid box of the art selection. They can use a variety of dot sizes, colors, and spacings to recreate shading, emphasis and definition.

6. **Collaboratively reimagine the original image.** Have students tape together their individual stippled grid boxes in a new way so that each grid box is part of one new piece of art. Students can then compare their reimagined composition with the original and identify how the stippling effected the overall piece. Alternatively, you can take a digital picture of each student grid box and then create a single piece using photo-editing software.

Essential Question: Why are parts important to the whole?

DRAMA

Drama is an area that is already so accessible in the reading classroom through Readers Theatre. In this section, we hope to showcase ways to go beyond the simple "go-to" strategies of Tableau and Readers Theatre to give you more depth in the STEM areas as a problem-seeking and problem-solving tool.

Human Flipbook

Theater Focus: Elements of action and imitation   **STEM Focus**: Present a possible solution to a problem through logical reasoning and communication

Lesson and Assessment Reference in Part 3: Interpreting Remainders (Grades 3-5)

Sequence:
The challenge to human flipbook is summarizing the key elements of the problem and solution into a single gesture and then sequencing that together seamlessly. By doing the strategy in two segments (once for the problem and once for the solution), students are able to visually identify and connect the parallels between them. By allowing the audience time to write down what they see, the brain has time to process the big rocks of the problem and its subsequent suggested

solution. Additionally, the audience could move the key segments around to change the order in both the problem and the solution flipbook to actually see the effects. You can also have students digitally document each gesture through a picture or still video and stitch them together to create a stop animation film. Many applications work for this, but at the present time the Vine app and Animoto are great options.

1. **Select a piece of text or word problem** you would like students to explore.

2. **Have the class summarize and sequence the problem,** using descriptive vocabulary which acts as a prompt for inquiry.

3. **Select a key detail** in each sequence and underline this word.

4. **Break the class into small groups** - 1 for each sequence in the summary and a group that is the audience- and have them examine the key detail and how they would like to portray that detail in a single gesture.

5. **Have students practice their chosen gesture in a frozen stance.** While this is happening, gather the audience together and ask them to look for facial expressions, body stance and energy levels of each group. They will notate what they see for each group. The audience should create a chart for each element they are noticing to make this process easier.

6. **Student groups will then perform their frozen gestures in order like a flip book.** When ready, the teacher will line up each group in order. The first group will perform their frozen gesture on the word "action". When the teacher says "FLIP!" the next group will immediately move into their frozen

gesture. Give the audience enough time to jot down what they see for each category.

7. **Continue this process** until the entire summary sequence has been performed.

8. **Repeat step 6, but this time say "FLIP!" every 3 seconds.** The audience does not need to write anything down this time, but should instead be observing the sequence coming together.

9. **Repeat step 8, but wait only 1 second between each FLIP.**

10. **Repeat steps 4-9, but this time focus on a solution.** Match up each key piece of the solution to the original sequence and present the "solution flip book" in this order.

Essential Question: How does sequencing help us to interpret and solve problems?

If/Then

(As shared by Arts Integration Specialist Deirdre Moore)

Theater Focus: Use of space, body and voice elements   **STEM Focus**: Draw a conclusion or prediction based upon evidence

Lesson and Assessment Reference in Part 3: Reactive Fireworks (Grades 6-8)

Sequence:

This strategy is so aligned to the scientific and engineering process that it is a natural fit for STEM. Essentially, you are focusing on cause and effect through experimentation. What makes this strategy so helpful is that students don't know what the "then" part of the question will be. They must take what they have constructed through their own experience and conclude or predict how a suggested outcome may manifest itself.

1. **Pick 2 or more elements from any piece of text or word problem** you are working on with your students.

2. **Assign each student one of the elements** and ask them to read a select portion of text which describes that element. This may be one or two words that surround an element, or a full description.

3. **Ask students to write down words** that would describe the outcome of their assigned element based upon their investigation of the surrounding text. Then, have them pick their top three and circle them.

4. **Prepare students for their drama experience** by having them practice using only their bodies to show each of their three descriptive words. Share their depictions with a partner.

5. **Once students are ready, ask each student to come up front.** As the teacher/director, explain that you will ask them an "if/then" question. The "if" part of the question will use one of their descriptive words. They would need to depict this word with their bodies like they practiced. The teacher/

director will then provide the "then" part of the question and students will need to show how their character would respond to that "then."

Example: "If the leaf was wilting, then what would happen if you added water?"

Essential Question: How does prior knowledge help us to predict a future outcome?

Build-a-Character

Theater Focus: Use of energy and improvisation   **STEM Focus**: Interpret and communicate STEM information

Lesson and Assessment Reference in Part 3: Character Shapes (Grades K-2)

Sequence:
Typically, this strategy is used when breaking apart a text, play or film. However, using it to bring characterization to something like a shape, a word problem, or a concept in the STEM areas allows for a whole shift in the way students think about this topic. That shift moves students from concrete to abstract and then back to concrete thinking, which in turn helps them to interpret and make meaning surrounding a topic or idea.

1. **Choose a shape, element or concept to depict as a character** from a selected piece of text, concept or word problem.

2. **Ask students to think about** what that character's (aka: shape, element or concept) facial expression, body movement, gestures, voice and energy level might look like.

3. **Explore each of these areas as a class** for the character and then perform these elements together with the teacher as the narrator. The teacher could say "Iron's facial expression says..." and then students can perform that selected element. Continue until all elements have been explored.

4. **Select another character from the text or concept and break students into 5 small groups.** Each group is assigned one of the elements to explore and create for that character.

5. **Gather all of the groups together into a large circle.** When the teacher narrates the character prompt (ie: "a square's facial expression says..."), that group will stand in their spots on the circle and perform their element. The teacher narrator will immediately move into the next element, until all of the elements of the character have been dramatized.

Essential Question: How do we make meaning of complex elements, ideas or text?

MUSIC

Often considered one of the most difficult arts areas for integration, this section will provide you with easily accessible and practical solutions for bringing in music with integrity to any classroom.

Play and Tell

Music Focus: Analysis   **STEM Focus**: Defining problems and designing solutions

Lesson and Assessment Reference in Part 3: Producing Beats (Grades 9-12)

Sequence:
The purpose of the Play and Tell exercise is to discover how students think about a topic or problem and their process for working through that topic or problem. The key to this lies not within the instrument or sound they choose, but rather the three sentences that they create to describe the instrument or sound. The music is the medium through which they express their thinking process.

1. **Select a large topic** you'd like to discuss or focus upon, such as the mathematical functions, the investigative practice, or creating algorithms.

2. **Ask students to work in pairs or small groups** to think about what sound or instrument would represent that thematic focus.

3. **Once they select or create their sound/instrument,** ask students to think of 3 sentences to describe why that sound or instrument best showcases the idea.

4. **Finally, have students create and perform their sound f**or the larger group while their partner acts as a narrator and shares the 3 sentences surrounding the sound.

Essential Question: How do we interpret ideas?

Improvisation Frame

Music Focus: Analysis   **STEM Focus**: Experimentation and Collaboration

Lesson and Assessment Reference in Part 3: Musical Fractions (Grades 3-5)

Sequence:
Improvisation is the foundation for composition, yet it can be an area that is not given a lot of attention is general music classes. This strategy provides a framework to allow for exploration and improvisation which helps ease the anxiety of both students and teachers. By providing a few structured pieces and then allowing students to mix and match, they are able to be successful in their

compositions and learn through the process how to use what they know to create a whole new product.

1. **Create a "frame" of students.** Rather than asking students to form a circle, ask them to form a rectangle or square. This becomes your human frame.

2. **Assign** each side a specific musical rhythmic value, element (forte or piano), or process (crescendo, diminuendo).

3. **Ask one student to move** to the center of the frame.

4. **The student in the center needs to improvise a 4-8 beat phrase using only the pieces that make up the frame.** For instance, if your frame represents musical rhythmic values and one side is a quarter note, one side is an eighth note, one side is a quarter rest and one side is a sixteenth note, those are the only note values the student in the center can choose for their improvisation.

5. **The frame performs their assigned element, skill or process** while the student in the center performs their 4-8 beat improvisation. Once the student is finished, they may choose another student to take their place.

Essential Question: Why do we experiment?

Round and Round

Music Focus: Form, Active listening   **STEM Focus**: Problem-solving and Perseverance

Lesson and Assessment Reference in Part 3: Form and Observation (Grades K-2)

Sequence:
Rounds are a musical form that require one group to start a piece and the other group to come in at a later designated time using the same music. Example: Sing "Are you sleeping?" in your head. In a round, one group would start the song and when they got to the part that says "brother John", the other group would start "Are you sleeping". One group will end after the other.

1. **Practice performing a simple round** like Are You Sleeping with your students.

2. **Once students are used to the concept of a round, clap a simple 4-beat pattern** (IE: clap, tap-tap, clap, tap-tap). Have all students echo the pattern. Add words that match your pattern (IE: You're hap-py, I'm hap-py) and have all students echo.

3. **Continue adding patterns** until you have a 4 phrase (sentence) composition.

4. **Once students know the whole composition, split them into two groups** and perform their composition as a round.

5. **Continue to split the class into smaller groups to make the round more complicated** (3 groups, 4 groups, etc). As students struggle, encourage them to listen to their team and then to the whole group to find their way back into the round.

Essential Question: How do we individually and collaboratively work to solve problems?

DANCE

Did you know that many of our minority populations, boys and special education students respond more positively to movement than any other strategy? Don't let dance intimidate you; try these strategies the next time you feel frustrated with reaching ALL of your students.

Movement Vocabulary

Dance Focus: Create and Communicate Meaning   **STEM Focus**: Interpret and Communicate STEM Information

Lesson and Assessment Reference in Part 3: Moving Constellations (Grades 3-5)

Sequence:

Vocabulary is a key feature in any content area. Though we sometimes associate it with language arts, vocabulary acquirement and deep understanding is actually at the heart of fluency in any content area. By focusing on using the arts to connect and make meaning to STEM content vocabulary, students are better able to grasp these terms in application.

1. **Create a list of vocabulary words** you would like students to explore. Alternative: ask students for a list of current vocabulary words they are struggling to remember or understand.

2. **Ask students for a synonym** for each word that would describe the original vocabulary word (ie: continent = one of 7 large land masses).

3. **Choose one of the words; let students know what that word is and that you will be playing a piece of music.** They will need to move around the room however the music makes them feel, but when the music stops, they will need to freeze their bodies in a way that represents that word.

4. **Repeat step 3 until all of the words have been chosen** and students have been able to freeze into its "body definition."

Essential Question: How do we make vocabulary visible?

Minute to Limit

Dance Focus: Elements of Body and Shape   **STEM Focus**: Collaborate as a STEM Team to problem-solve

Lesson and Assessment Reference in Part 3: Bubble Solution (Grades K-2)

Sequence:
This strategy uses various limitations, including time, to force students to think creatively, critically and collaboratively to solve an overarching problem. It provides students much-needed practice in thinking on their feet using the elements of movement.

1. **Choose a content standard and a naturally aligned dance standard.**

2. **Focus on what dance element would be the target** used to achieve the desired learning outcome of the dance standard. For example, if you've chosen the movement standard of "identifying and demonstrating movement elements and skills in performing dance," select a dance element such as shape or space to use as a pathway to teaching that standard.

3. **Embed a learning activity to teach the content standard through the arts element.** For example, if you are using the dance elements identified above to help teach geometric shapes, you can have students create a specific shape like a pentagon as a group of 3 people (limiting people compared to sides).

4. **After students can master the first activity, then take something else away in addition to the first item.** For example, this time try taking away the ability to talk about how they will make the shape, as well as only working in groups of 3.

5. **Finally, limit the time they are able to use their element to demonstrate their understanding.** For example, in addition to only being in a group of 3 and not being able to speak about the activity, limit students to only having 20 seconds to create their designated shape.

Essential Question: How do limitations effect problem-solving?

Book "Marking"

Dance Focus: Choreography **STEM Focus**: Engaging in logical reasoning

Lesson and Assessment Reference in Part 3: Decoding daVinci (Grades 9-12)

Sequence:
Marking is a strategy dancers use to walk through a dance without actually going through a full-blown performance. This minimization of the dance steps requires more focus and still provides the coach or instructor with feedback into the sequence that a dancer has in their mind. By applying this strategy to a STEM concept or complex task, you can identify strengths and challenges in information processing by your students.

1. **Provide students with a large piece of complex text,** such as a set of lab instructions or a multi-step math word problem.

2. **Have students select pieces of the text that they would like to bookmark** as a key detail they would like to remember. They may bookmark as many places as they would like.

3. **For each bookmarked area,** students should select a movement that they could perform that represents that key detail.

4. **Have students practice performing** the full movement they chose for their bookmark.

5. **Then, students should minimize that movement so that they restrain the range of motion.** For instance, if they chose a turning motion to represent a rotation, instead of turning all the way around, they could stand in place and simply rotate their head. They should be able to perform their "marked" motion while seated at their desk.

6. **Repeat step 5 for each area** they have bookmarked.

Essential Question: Why do we use steps to help us process information?

Mirroring

Dance Focus: Elements of Body and Space **STEM Focus**: Collaborate, Interpret and Communicate STEM information

Lesson and Assessment Reference in Part 3: Dancing Angles (Grades 6-8)

Sequence:

Mirroring is a strategy that is used widely in many different areas. It has been found that when humans mirror the actions of another, they build trust and can even influence their partner's actions and reactions. When used appropriately in math and engineering, the effects of mirroring on comprehension and problem-solving practice can be dramatic. The key to this version of the strategy lies in the moment when students have to transfer leadership to their partner and when they can no longer see their partner. This heightens their other senses and forces them to find solutions that might otherwise have not presented themselves.

1. **Pair students** and have them stand across from each other. Ask students to choose one person to be the leader and another to be the follower.

2. **The leader will begin to move** their arms and legs while remaining grounded by their central body axis. Their partner will need to mirror the action of the leader (i.e.: left hand goes up, the follower's right hand will also go up). You may provide a context such as "only move in right angles" or you may allow them to move freely with the central stationary axis - meaning that their core doesn't move, but their arms and legs can move.

3. **Once successfully completed, have students switch roles.** The follower now gets a chance to be the leader and moves to explore all of the surrounding space while maintaining a stationary body axis.

4. **Repeat step 2, but this time the leader needs to pass the leadership role to the follower** without telling the follower that it is their turn. The follower will need to feel when the leader is passing the leadership role onto them, accept it, and become the new leader.

5. **Once both partners have had a chance to be the leader, have them turn around back-to-back.** Repeat the same activity, but this time the partners will need to mirror one another without seeing the motion. They will need to rely completely on their senses of touch and hearing to determine what and how to mirror.

Essential Question: What role do senses play in our interpretation of the world?

Chapter Review

Strategies for accessing the arts authentically in the STEM areas are an important piece to being able to use STEAM effectively with your students. The strategies presented in this book are only 14 samples to get you started. There are certainly many more arts strategies that can be utilized effectively in the classroom which connect broadly with STEM concepts and I encourage you to seek them out. Hopefully, you are now able to see how multiple art forms can be used to engage your students in STEAM learning and can activate their critical thinking and creativity skills. Take this opportunity to reflect upon the chapter using the following questions:

1. How do you differentiate between a strategy and a lesson?

2. What are your celebrations and concerns about the strategy foundations that have been outlined in this chapter?

3. Which strategy presented in this chapter is your favorite and why?

4. Which strategy presented in this chapter is your least favorite and why?

part 2 | from strategies to instruction

chapter 4 | s.t.e.a.m. behaviors

Desiree is on fire. She has just finished developing a new game that is elegantly simple in its design but addictive to play. She should know - she has just spent the last 5 hours testing it out with her friends online and it felt like 5 minutes. The concept is easy: maneuver falling notes into positions that will play a familiar song before time runs out on the screen. Think of a mashup between old-school Tetrus and Candy Crush with music. Time is always running out, though, and the better you get, the faster the clock counts down.

Desiree is content; the game is fun to play and you can even work through it in a group mode that she and her friends came up with after a few days of messing around with the code. She uploads it to several app libraries online and gives it away for free. After all, creating it was just something fun to do and now, others can enjoy it too. Plus, by giving it away for free, she'll receive much more feedback and find out if there are any bugs that she needs to work out. She closes her laptop and climbs into bed to get some sleep before the alarm goes off for school the next morning.

Desiree is 13.

There are students like Desiree in every school and classroom in the world. Do you understand her? Do you know what makes her tick? If we are simply providing the Desirees of the world with Algebra I or Pre-Calculus classes but not teaching these concepts in ways that capitalize on all of the background knowledge and experiences our students possess, we have missed the mark. And what's even more troubling than missing the mark is not understanding the unique qualities of the 21st century arrows that sit in our classrooms.

Let's take a deeper look at Desiree and the insights into her student profile that we can glean from the brief story provided. Obviously, she is a young girl who is probably in 8th or 9th grade. She has a sophisticated knowledge of how to use technology as a tool for creation. What's more, she must have some knowledge (and probably a high-level of understanding) of how to utilize code to develop a game from scratch and edit it based upon user feedback. And, she understands how to market, evaluate and revise her idea to a wide audience. But this is all just what can be gathered about her on the surface.

Underneath this exterior are the underlying foundations of what Desiree comes into her morning classes knowing and being able to do. She has a self-motivated desire to learn and grow. In order to learn how to code a game, it takes a lot of trial and error. You begin with a few simple lines of code to see what happens when you change one or two elements. Then, you slowly begin to learn how each element of the coding language can have an effect on some aspect of what you are creating. This is not an easy process, so we know that she is also someone who perseveres through the problem-solving process. It takes many lines of code to create just one action, and one wrong keystroke can cause the whole program to go haywire. So, she must also pay close attention to detail, seek out any errors and work through potential solutions. Desiree is not just a problem-solver; she is also a problem-seeker.

Additionally, Desiree values collaboration with others. How do we know this? Because she didn't develop the game in isolation. She tested it out with her network of friends, heard their feedback and adjusted some elements of the game to include a group mode. Plus, she placed it online for free so that anyone could download it and provide her with feedback. She understands the value in building trust with an audience, learning from their input and making a better product. Desiree is also savvy enough to know that the first iteration of an idea is probably not the best one and having others discover the natural bugs will save her time in the long run and make the idea that much stronger.

Does the fact that she is 13 surprise you? It shouldn't. Today's students are the most technologically self-sourced learners in the history of the world. If they want to know something - anything - they can with the click of a button or a swipe of the screen. If they want to learn something, they know that they simply need to take their knowledge and put it into practice. What are we providing to service these students? Certainly, it cannot just be devices nor can it be a technology class. As prices continue to go down for technology, more and more students will have access to the incredible potential that the internet provides: knowledge from anywhere for anything. And while it is true that rural areas are still struggling to gain equitable access to the internet and technology, that does not necessarily translate into no STEAM knowledge or skills. The crux of the STEAM process lies within the concepts of inquiry, exploration, discovery and creation which doesn't require connection to a single piece of technology. We must get the idea of devices and access to technology as equating to STEM and STEAM out of our heads!

Instead, it is time to shift **how** we are teaching to ensure that **what** we are teaching is relevant to our learners. Just because students can learn algebra, biology or coding online doesn't mean that we should not still be teaching it as a class. What it does mean is that educators must become facilitators of learning experiences and create opportunities for students to understand the connections across and through these areas of study. Students still need to learn the skills, but we have done them a tremendous disservice by not providing a way for students to apply those skills in meaningful ways that are relevant to their backgrounds and interests.

This chapter will focus on what behaviors best assist our students through the STEAM process and how to leverage these behaviors to ensure that the learning is at the deepest levels possible. These behaviors represent three key drivers to STEAM teaching and learning which lead to a greater understanding of our students and their learning characteristics. It's time for a reboot.

Coding Characteristics

Rebooting our behaviors is much like giving a computer program a fresh start. Sometimes this just requires a moment of rest, but sometimes, this means creating new lines of code that will clean up the virus and give your application new life. The basics of coding a computer program, application, or website are fairly simple: for every line of code that you enter, the computer program, application or website will perform an action. Coding is at its core a language which can be spoken and responded to in a logical sequence. If we were to take a look at the definition for Code in the dictionary, we would find the following:

code *noun* \ˈkōd\

1: a systematic statement of a body of law; *especially* : one given statutory force

2: a system of principles or rules <moral *code*>

3a : a system of signals or symbols for communication

3b : a system of symbols (as letters or numbers) used to represent assigned and often secret meanings

4: <u>genetic code</u>

5: a set of instructions for a computer

Number five is what we're really interested in here, but take a look at the other four definitions of code as a noun. All of them relate in some way to the basic idea that a code is a system, much like language is a communication system. In translation to a STEAM approach, understanding that the process of STEAM is a language for communication is critical to its success. *What* we communicate must be translated congruently by our students in order for them to respond and create their own learning. Therefore, it may help us to understand the definition of code in its form as a verb:

^{2}code *verb*

: to put (a message) into the form of a code so that it can be kept secret

: to mark (something) with a code so that it can be identified

: to change (information) into a set of letters, numbers, or symbols that can be read by a computer

Clearly, coding as a verb represents the communication, translation and application of your message based upon a system that is mutually agreed upon by two or more parties. To extrapolate this to teaching through a STEAM approach, both the teacher and the student must communicate through the use of a mutually-agreed upon system of teaching and learning. To do this, teachers must know their students' background knowledge, interests, strengths and gaps in order to best facilitate a learning experience. Conversely, students must know their teacher's expectations for learning, the intention for the learning experience and how that learning experience will be delivered. Both parties must calibrate their communication system to align with the proposed outcomes.

To determine your communication calibration, the I/T Belief statement exercise is often helpful. This is an extension of the If/Then strategy that was shared in Chapter 3. In this version, you perform the exercise with your students as a participant and facilitator, rather than as a sage from the stage. This helps for both you as the teacher and your students to understand each other's belief and expectation systems and to better align your STEAM process code.

Similar to the idea in computer programming that for every line of code expressed an action will be performed, in this exercise you begin by stating, "If you believe that...." which prompts the resolution of "then...." a certain action is expected or performed. For instance, if you begin this exercise with your students by saying "If you believe that I should embrace your use of cell phones in class, then...." and ask them what you could expect from them in that scenario. What would be the effect of opening up your class to their use of mobile devices from the student point of view? This will give you incredible insights into not only their thinking, but also the possibilities that they create through their response. Then, for each "then" statement, add another "if" proposal. For example, if the response to your first prompt was "...then we could look up information faster," continue the exercise with "If you could look up information faster, then...." and continue down the rabbit hole. The idea is that for every code you enter with your "if" statement, the response from the students will elicit a new line of code for you to explore until you reach the root behaviors that will be agreed upon in your class or school.

Don't stop there, though, because that would make this calibration one-sided. Once you have explored an idea, behavior, or expectation in this way with your students from your perspective, turn the tables. Now it's time for your students to present you with the "If" prompts so that you can respond with the outputs that prompt would elicit given your own distinct blend of teaching experiences, background, and expectations. Just as you learned an incredible amount of information about your students' motivation, background knowledge, and which direction they would like to go, so too will your students learn about you and your unique teaching style.

Hopefully, you can see the by-products of this kind of exercise. There are a myriad of possibilities that if/then belief statements can lead to when used to help explore, discover and guide instructional practices and opportunities. The very nature of this process encompasses what we hope to achieve with the STEAM approach itself, which is to provide students with experiences that prompt their inquiry, enhance their skills, apply their knowledge and create a new solution. Not only can you use this exercise to structure your own STEAM class, but it can be a foundational process that can be applied to the various learning experiences you hope to implement. Additionally, this same process of if/then is what all artists use to explore the world and to transform their understanding of the world into new creative works. By understanding and utilizing coding characteristics interwoven with the artistic process, STEAM-based learning truly has a chance to take root and grow.

Student-led vs. Student-fed

One of the many professional development activities that I use with educators is the packed, unpack, repack model of lesson exploration. In this example, we take an exemplar STEAM or Arts Integration lesson and I model it for the participants. If we are able, I try to present the lesson to an actual class of students so that the participating educators can see the lesson in action, write down their observations through a guided peer review sheet, and then reflect upon what they saw in a later session with me. If this isn't possible, then the professional development participants become my students and engage in the lesson with me as the instructional facilitator.

Next, I provide them with the opportunity to reflect on the lesson design, implementation, and process alone and then invite them to share their reflections with a colleague. We then come back together to discuss common themes that emerged, questions that arose, and those wonderful "ah-ha" moments. At this point, we dig deeply into the lesson itself and discuss why each part is present and best practices for its use and delivery. Then, I break the large group into smaller subgroups of 2-4 people and assign each group a piece of the lesson. These subgroups are given the task to teach their selection to the group at large in sequenced order. Therefore, the group that has the pre-engagement will go first, followed by the group that has the engagement portion of the lesson and so on. They are all given up to 5 minutes to plan how they will teach their portion of the lesson to the larger group and are encouraged to work with the groups surrounding their lesson portion to ensure a smooth flow to the lesson at large.

Finally comes my favorite part: the repackage portion of the exercise. It is here where I as the facilitator learn the most about the educators in the room. Each subgroup must present their portion of the lesson (which may be modified to highlight things they may feel to be more important) in sequence so that by the end of the time the entire lesson has been retaught by the participants of the session. This is beneficial to the teachers because they are permitted to play with the lesson without fear of getting it "wrong," and teachers will notice their own gaps through their colleagues. This is beneficial to me as the facilitator because I can immediately get a sense for whether each teacher operates under the "student-led" model or the "student-fed" model of teaching practice.

Student-fed Model

In the student-fed model of instruction, teachers are the givers of information and the students are the recipients. Before dismissing the idea that you may fall into this category of teaching, keep in mind that giving information can take many forms. It doesn't always mean that you are standing in front of the room providing a lecture or a presentation. In fact, most of the time this isn't the case. Some of the very best teachers I have observed fall into the student-fed camp of instruction. That's because it is the way many of us learned how to teach way back when we were in college.

The student-fed model is anytime when you are providing the information for the student, rather than letting the student explore the idea on their own. This could mean a lecture or teaching via a presentation, but it could also look like any of these common activities:

- Explaining everything about an object, idea or concepts
- Asking questions to which there is a "right" answer
- Answering all questions that students ask
- Planning lessons based solely upon what is next in the curriculum guide

And there are many more that we could add to the list. If these examples make you a bit uncomfortable, then you are normal! We all do these things at one point or another and we can't make a blanket statement that says this is not a good model for instruction. There are times when it is absolutely necessary to provide our students with information in this manner. However, to develop truly STEAM-based learning behaviors, the shift of balance must move from student-fed to student-led.

Student-led Model

In the student-led model of instruction, students are in charge of their own learning and the teacher takes the role of instructional facilitator. This means that students are given opportunities to inquire and explore a concept to determine the pathway that they would like to take to better understanding the topic at hand. The teacher then provides key pieces of guidance and assists students in moving towards their goal of constructed meaning. This doesn't mean that there is a free-for-all in the classroom. Teachers are still selecting the topic of instruction and have a clear expectation of what standards students will be expected to know and do through an authentic assessment of learning. However, students have a greater role in how that learning occurs in a student-led model of instruction.

Student-led learning can also take on a variety of manifestations. It can be very open-ended if the teacher is comfortable with a broad level of latitude. This may mean that the teacher simply provides a topic and provides students with the tools necessary to begin to explore and research this topic and to determine which pathway they would like to use to move through the information. However, this is fairly uncommon due to both the ability to easily become off-task and lack of time for such a broad focus. What is much more typical in a student-led environment is when the teacher provides a topic, uses some thinking prompts to engage students in a narrowed focus of that topic and then provides students with the chance to interact and experiment with the information through learning activities that are aligned with their cognitive levels, interests, and background knowledge. To capture this idea, think about the following visual. If your students are taking a trip towards learning a concept or idea, they are the drivers and can use a map or GPS system to help guide them along their way to their end destination. As their teacher, you are the guardrails that keep them from sliding off the road. In a STEAM classroom, this could look like:

- Students who are experimenting with a musical instrument to describe how it makes sound

- Asking students questions which encourage divergent thinking

- Students doing more and sitting less

- Using reflective journaling to process and explain diverse and complex concepts

In these examples, the students take a much more hands-on role in their learning and because of this, they are more invested in the outcome of that learning. This leads to higher levels of engagement, a deeper level of connection with the skills and processes being attained and a better end-product. After all, an excellent product is hard to come by without an excellent process. And an excellent process can be developed over time through intentional and sequential acts of learning experiences.

A New Kind of Blended Learning

When the term "blended learning" appears, often it is in reference to learning information face-to-face and online in some combination. But a new kind of blended learning is taking shape through the STEAM approach. When looking at student-fed and student-led learning models, it shouldn't be a one-size-fits-all choice. Instead, the best kind of learning to facilitate the STEAM approach is one in which there is a blend of these two options. There will be times when it is necessary for teachers to feed information to students and provide them with some clear examples and specific tasks. There will also be times when a student-led, inquiry based approach is better suited to the learning experience based upon the desired outcome as it relates to the standards being taught. This is the beauty of using an integrated approach to teach these content areas: the teacher has the ability to craft a lesson where all participants are artisans.

How to blend these two types of learning models together is still up to the teacher and is dependent upon the variety of factors that effect any classroom. However, the shift of balance in an authentic STEAM-based approach would suggest a heavier emphasis on student-led instruction with student-fed instruction being used as needed to support and service the active learning taking place. When in doubt, ask yourself if students could explore that idea or concept actively rather than passively in the learning process and be successful. If so, give them the opportunity. If the answer is no, determine exactly what information you need to feed your students in order to empower them to move into student-led learning.

Intentional Actions

Finally, the final key behavior that ensures a vigorous and successful STEAM approach to learning is through intentional actions towards alignment and connections. This doesn't mean forcing connections, though intentional may be forceful in its connotation. Rather, this means that you are being purposeful in seeking out, aligning, teaching and assessing standards that make natural connections across content areas. This is by far, the piece that separates true STEAM integration from STEAM enhancement.

Acting with intention through the STEAM approach means that you are selecting standards that align in an equitable and elegant way with one another. You are doing this with the purpose of exploring both standards so that the learning of these standards in tandem with each other leads to a greater understanding of the overarching topic. This is not spur-of-the-moment opportunity that happens in your 4th period class on a Tuesday. Those moments are important, to be sure, and we must capitalize on them. But that is not intentional and therefore, doesn't provide a framework for the context of student learning.

By being intentional also means that how you teach both standards is thought-out and selected based upon the factors that you know to be at the heart of successful learning for your students. You have a clear and chosen pathway for facilitating student learning that is both flexible enough to allow for student discovery and yet resilient in its overarching guidelines. Moving through the lesson with intention also provides you with a barometer for student comprehension and allows you to be responsive to their needs. Should you need to deviate from the original plan, you are able to make that choice because you have plenty of options for assisting students in their learning exploration of the content.

Finally, being intentional with how you assess a lesson, topic or unit in a STEAM approach maintains the integrity and consistency with which the entire lesson has been carried out. Knowing not only what, but also how and why you will assess both standards provides you with a clear idea of the steps needed to move your students from the beginning to the end of the lesson in a way that supports the outcome necessitated by the standard. This ensures that your assessments are truly measuring the standards chosen from the very beginning and tightens up the structure of your lesson while maintaining the pliability that is necessary for inquiry-based learning. There is an ebb and flow to the STEAM approach that is representative of the natural learning process and which, when used purposefully, can deepen the entire course of learning for a child.

Chapter Review

In this chapter, we have explored three key behaviors that unlock successful outcomes in a STEAM approach: calibrating our communication, shifting the balance from student-led to student-fed learning models, and ensuring that we are intentional in our design, implementation and assessments of STEAM-based learning. Before moving on to the next chapter, take a moment to reflect upon what you've learned through these prompts:

1. What would your "If/Then" prompts be with your students?

2. How might student population effect the use of these three key behaviors?

3. Which learning model are you currently using: student-led or student-fed?How do you foresee blending these two models?

4. Why is intention important in a STEAM approach?

chapter 5 | building a s.t.e.a.m. community

case study #2

North Elementary School

Location: Cedar City, Utah

Profile:
- 469 students in grades Pre-K-5
- 54% receive Free and Reduced Meals
- Average class size is 26 students
- Title I School
- Student demographics include 75% Caucasian, 1% Black, 15% Hispanic, 3% Two or more races, and 5% American Indian/Alaska Native
- Community: Rural

STEAM Initiative Leaders:
Ray Whittier (Principal), Melanie Skankey (Arts Integration Specialist)

Timeframe:
2013-2014 is the third year of implementation.

Gathered in a circle on the floor of an arts classroom in Cedar City, Utah, a group of 4th graders are sharing their opinions on their recent Rock Cycle Infomercials. This "Talk Back" circle is one of their favorite parts of the lesson because they get the opportunity to share their own insights about the process of their learning. Their teacher, Ms. Skankey, gently prompts them with questions about their discoveries and their burning questions. She doesn't ask them for answers; she truly wants to help them work through all of the steps they went through in their infomercial productions. Each child provides a piece of their understanding, a question for another student group, or an idea for the teachers in the group to think about for the next lesson. Oh yes - their teachers are a part of this circle, too. Not as leaders, but as fellow learners who respect their students' insights into their own preferences and pathways for discovery.

This magical moment didn't come without a long road of trial and error, nor does it come without a price. North Elementary is a rural public elementary school that was struggling to retain enrollment in 2010. As so often happens in cases like this, the drop in enrollment from their school meant that surrounding schools were becoming overcrowded and understaffed. At the time, the school had hired one arts specialist to provide instruction for all students in visual arts, music, and theatre through a grant provided by the state legislature in the hopes that providing an arts program would boost engagement and attendance. As the population continued to dwindle, school leaders started taking a critical look at the root causes of the decline as well as research in ways that were proven to increase student achievement and close gaps. From this data analysis, it became clear that there needed to be a higher level of focus on improving their students' success in the fields of science and mathematics, in a way that made learning more meaningful.

In 2011, North Elementary made the decision to become a STEAM school in an effort to bring a cohesive integrated experience into their curriculum and culture. Still only able to provide one arts educator, Melanie Skankey, then became the arts integration specialist for the school. She was provided with professional development opportunities to learn how to integrate across content areas and leaned on resources from the Kennedy Center to help guide her understanding and implementation of an arts integrated approach.

Meanwhile, the rest of the school was starting from scratch. Administration clearly communicated the vision and mission of the shift to a STEAM approach and several educators in the building left in search of other positions that were more aligned with their teaching philosophies. Those who chose to stay made the conscious decision to learn about the integrated approach during their planning time and before and after school. Additionally, school leaders forged a partnership with a local university, Southern Utah University, to bring in teaching artists as models and partners in arts integrated instruction. Today, teachers continue to work side by side with these teaching artists in the implementation of arts integrated lessons that are focused on STEM topics and standards.

Creating Buy-In

"STEAM doesn't work unless everyone wants to be a part of it. You've got to have people who are all in," Melanie emphatically remarks when asked about what makes a successful STEAM implementation. She goes on to explain that the process took a lot of effort during the first year, mainly due to the fact that everyone needed a foundational understanding of integration, the arts' role in STEAM, and planning for that elegant fit.

Melanie continues by saying, "that first year, I would plan with each team 60 minutes, two or three times a month. It was a lot of work up front," though this planning was fluid and dependent upon what the grade-level teams were working on at the time. This became a critical piece for creating teacher buy-in because Melanie was flexible with when and how she was supporting each team.

"Most of the time, I planned with these groups before or after school since the regular school day schedule didn't allow for collaborative planning between our areas," Melanie explained. This is common with many schools who are trying on an integration approach. That kind of flexibility is key to building teacher commitment to the process. Classroom teachers can see that the arts specialist is giving up their time and talents to help support them in their own professional needs and growth. Meanwhile, the arts specialist can build stronger advocates for dedicated arts time through more directed conversations with their classroom teacher counterparts. Both build a mutual respect for the scope and complexities of their comparable curricular content standards.

Now, the planning time is much more fluid as more teachers have become comfortable with the integration process. Melanie may only plan with teams for 30 or 60 minutes once a month, depending on what they are working on. More often, Melanie will have a brief conversation on what topics are coming up that they could use as a way to build a new STEAM experience and then either she or the teachers will create a lesson based on this short collaboration. Additionally, because they invested in the planning time up front three years ago, they have a library of successful lessons that they can use or tweak to teach that same concept to a new class of students each year. This saves them time and allows them to explore new ways to approach other topics that haven't been broached before.

Another way that Melanie suggests for creating buy-in is through integrating with areas that teachers are interested in, or which capitalize on their own strengths. Several teachers who were whizzes at technology used that as their starting point and Melanie used that in the collaborative development of their lessons. Others excelled at visual arts, which is not Melanie's area of focus (she has a degree in theatre) so together, they leveraged these strengths to produce an integrated lesson using the visual arts standards. When using an area of comfort, teachers are much less likely to be resistant because teaching and learning is fun for them, which in turn helps to build the excitement for learning in their students.

Finally, Melanie recommends using student surveys to highlight the areas of interest, the highest-impact of a lesson and student reflections on their own learning to help bring other teachers on board. When students can share their own perspectives about what is most meaningful for them, teachers are more inclined to want to use those methods in their teaching. Most teachers truly have a desire to engage their students and activate their learning. When they are aware of what students need and want in their learning experience, teachers are more driven to use these strategies.

STEAM Approach

The structure behind North Elementary's approach to STEAM uses what resources they have at their disposal, while maintaining as much integrity to their arts program as possible. While having a full-time visual art, music and theatre teacher would be recommended, this is not part of their current reality. With that in mind, here are a few key elements to how STEAM is being integrated through the curriculum at North:

Lesson Planning

Lesson planning still happens before or after school, and is typically scheduled for once per month. Grade-level teams work with Melanie to create STEAM units

(Integrated Curriculum Units) which may be done in either the classroom or during one of the arts class periods. During these planning sessions, there is an emphasis on finding high-quality fits between the standards and assessments to ensure a tightly integrated lesson experience. The intention is not to integrate all STEAM elements in a lesson, but rather to have a STEAM focus in a unit. Typically, the focus centers around a science topic which then branches into other areas using essential questions as a guide. While many teachers could do this lesson planning alone, they choose to collaborate with Melanie to ensure they are maintaining the integrity of the arts area being woven in and through the lesson.

Instruction

Melanie meets with each class twice per week for 45 minutes each time. In most instances, one of these class periods is reserved for dedicated arts instruction, while the other may be used as an integrated lesson. Melanie strongly believes that "there has to be foundational arts skills" in order for STEAM integration to occur with authenticity. To her, this means that students are learning the arts skills first in isolation and then applying those skills organically through an integrated lesson that teaches the focused topics in and through the arts.

While approximately half of Melanie's time is dedicated in integration, classroom teachers are not absent from this equation. Often, teachers are engaged in the integrated lesson either through co-teaching a concept in the integrated lesson, or by teaching their own STEAM lesson during their regular classroom time. All teachers at North Elementary provide integrated lessons in their own classrooms at least twice per month.

Ongoing Professional Learning

Teachers at North Elementary are active participants in collaborative peer professional learning communities. These are mixed grade and content level teams that are charged with supporting the growth of the colleagues through Peer Reviews and Collaborative Lesson Debriefs. Each group observes each other every other month and completes a peer review of their colleague. They look for things like aligned standards, high quality teaching strategies, authentic learning experiences, and meaningful assessments and then bring their observations back in a non-threatening collaborative discussion. Additionally, these PLCs provide the teachers with a way to review each others' STEAM lessons to ensure both accountability and a spotlight on staying true to the mission and vision of the initiative.

Opportunities and Obstacles

As North Elementary now has three years of experience in the use of a STEAM approach, they have discovered their own unique set of triumphs and challenges along the way. For example, when starting this kind of initiative, Melanie learned that sending articles about the benefits of integration and some strategies for inclusion didn't work. "Nobody read them," she said, not because they didn't want to but because no one had the time. Face-to-face collaboration and professional development is a much better approach when working through integration. Additionally, having teachers be a part of the learning experiences, like the Talk Back Circles, is far better than simply explaining it to them or sharing out during a staff meeting. Teachers respond better when they are witnessing the "ah-ha" moments of their students for themselves.

Another key piece to keep in mind is to introduce STEAM in small doses. "Don't do too much your first year," Melanie advises. Instead, she recommends building up to the process of integration using small but purposeful steps in that direction. Introduce one idea at a time and focus on consistency. Don't worry about collecting data right away; instead, ensure that everyone is using STEAM with integrity so that your data is valid and reliable when you do begin to perform some action research.

Additionally, be aware that not everyone will be on board right away, and this could include your parent community. "When we first started this, parents wanted to know why we were wasting our time on this arts stuff. They considered it fluff because when they thought of STEM or STEAM, they perceived this as a way to help their child to become a scientist, not a dancer. We needed to do a lot of work in better communicating the benefits of STEAM and what the arts bring to the table," Melanie shared. Lesson learned? Share the intention, benefits, and reasons why you are using STEAM with all stakeholders early on. Be clear in all communications about the purpose of STEAM, how you are using the approach and what evidence of learning parents should look for when their child is at home. Sharing the student surveys with parents is also a plus, as they can indicate lower behavioral issues and higher attendance rates due to greater engagement, as was the case at North Elementary.

Finally, a big part of getting the teachers to buy in to integrating the arts is how it affects students' attitude about school and the school's overall energy. Art makes people, not just students, happy. Teachers are active participants during STEAM units; they are not just sitting back and watching. Instead, they play the instruments or help with the painting or join in the theatre games. It adds to the positive energy in the class because no one feels too intimidated to play and experiment, not even the teachers. That's been a big part of how STEAM works for North. Melanie explained that "It's not like, well its art time the students are Mrs. Mel's problem. Or, you're doing math and that's not art so I won't help you. The students belong to both of us and both the art teacher and classroom teacher want to see them succeed everywhere."

Lesson Sample

The following is a lesson, shared by Melanie Skankey, as an example of one way in which integration is used at North. Please note that this is the follow up lesson to a dedicated theatre lesson done previously, which is in congruence with their belief that the arts skills are equally important in the integration process and should not be ignored. The skills students would have worked on in the previous lesson are as follows:

1. Students will experiment with different laban movements (twist, bend, flick, float)
2. Students will use a combination of laban movements to create a character
3. Students will portray a variety of characters using diverse movement

4th Grade Lesson

North Elementary School, Cedar City, UT
Melanie Skankey, Arts Integration Specialist

Science Objective	Drama Objective
Students will recognize instances of weathering and erosion.	Students will use expressive movement to portray characters traits

Joint Lesson Objective: Students will use personification to create scenes that demonstrate weathering or erosion

Warm-up
1. Grouping game

Weathering vs Erosion

1. Discuss the difference between the two. Make a list of processes that cause these events
2. Today we are going to create stories to demonstrate these process as if they were humans rather then parts of nature

Review/explain Personification

1. Personification is giving human traits to non human things such as water, wind, trees, etc
2. Actors can portray these non human characters by thinking about what human traits match the nonhuman characters
3. Using drum movement help students portray non human characters of lightning, turtle, rose
4. List scientific facts about lightning. Ask students how each trait might become a human characteristic
5. Use drum to try moving as humans with those traits

A Story of Weathering and Erosion:

1. Pick two characters that help with weathering
2. The problem in the scene is that a rock is weathering
3. The solution is that a character must use erosion to move the rock
4. Do a quick example

Character creation

1. Assign students either a weathering or erosion element
2. Have them list 3 scientific truths about that element
3. Change those into human traits that can be acted
4. Weathering line: must say at some point weathering and erosion

Collect and narrate: 10 mins

1. Pair teams together to stage with teacher providing narration
2. Give feedback on movements of character

Conclusion

Starting a STEAM initiative from scratch can present both excitement and trepidation. Being able to navigate through the waters of this integrated approach requires professional development, a commitment to a mission and vision for STEAM, and a sequential approach with a long-range time span. Nothing is a quick fix, and this needs to be shared openly and honestly from the beginning with all stakeholders of the school community. Additionally, no situation is ever perfect. Using the resources you have in a way that maintains the integrity of the arts while simultaneously using them to spur innovative critical thinking skills and processes is a challenge all on its own. Yet if you can capture a way to leverage them together, as North Elementary is doing, authentic student learning is indeed possible.

chapter 6 | s.t.e.a.m. environments

In the spring of 2012, Joseph "Jody" Giles, then CIO from Under Armour, Inc., came to be the keynote speaker at an Arts Integration EdCamp event that I helped to coordinate for Anne Arundel County Public Schools. When he bounded into the building at 8AM to set up his computer, he was wearing a pair of jeans, a white polo and a navy blue blazer with the Under Armour logo emblazoned on the left lapel. And of course, he was wearing a pair of Under Armour sneakers. His talk was centered around a simple concept: why we are all artisans. And while he exuded "cool" from the moment he began to speak until the last rousing refrain of encouragement, it wasn't his charisma that captured the audience. It was his description of the Under Armour team.

Under Armour, Inc. has developed performance athletic gear for the past 18 years - a relative newcomer to the athletics apparel business. The apparel has been worn by athletes of all varieties - from youth to professionals - and Under Armour has worked hard to collaborate with other STEM-based industries to revolutionize their product. To say that the company is innovative is an understatement. The foundation of their success lies in the original idea from founder Kevin Plank to develop a T-shirt that would "wick away sweat, support muscles and keep athletes cool and dry in the heat." In 1996, their first piece of athletic apparel, the Compression T-Shirt, was born and the company hasn't halted ever since. With over $2 billion in revenue, Under Armour is an American dream story. But behind every dream, there's a team propelling that dream towards a closer reality.

During his speech, Jody shared images from inside their company walls that showcased what a high-performing organization looks and acts like in order to create innovative solutions in the 21st century. We saw pictures of white boards covered with sketches for product ideas, the testing facilities that they use for their prototypes, even the basketball court where people go to play a round of hoops to clear their heads and keep healthy at the same time. It was fascinating to see the inner workings of a company that clearly placed value on both individual talents and how those talents could be added to the collective team of the organization. Each member of the Under Amour team has a role to play and the communication across the team allows for ideas to be explored and innovative solutions to be developed. It doesn't matter if you are a product tester, a designer, a marketer, or the Senior Vice President. Everyone needs to be an artist in their role in order for the team to be successful. Welcome to the future: this is how STEAM manifests itself in the global 21st century economy.

According to a 2011 article from the New York Times, the future of our success lies in innovation. This is "the crucial ingredient in all economic progress--higher growth for nations, more competitive products for companies, and more prosperous careers for individuals." In fact, in a 2010 report by the Corporate Executive board, companies who were reported as highly innovative had a "76 percent product success ration verses a 54 percent for companies with medium or low effectiveness ratings". Obviously, both being innovative and engaging in innovative tasks and activities is a critical element of success in the world today.

How are we preparing our students for this reality? By placing them in desks, which are either in rows or in groups of 4, pushed together around a classroom? In providing laptops to every child in the hopes that because technology is in their hands they will somehow magically turn it into something new? At this point, I hope you know where I am going with this. In order for the basic principles and processes of STEAM that have been shared thus far to take root, we must explore and create environments where these principles and practices can flourish. STEAM cannot live in a single classroom or in a lesson plan. It is a livable, flexible practice that must be allowed to transform the entire culture and learning habitat of a school. Think of it as the ivy that spreads around the walls of your home. STEAM should be interlacing itself everywhere in your building and to do that, you'll need some practical pillars for creating a STEAM environment.

The Studio/Lab Design

As you begin to create a space where STEAM can grow and thrive, you'll need to begin to think about classrooms very differently. Most people associate a classroom with desks and chairs, a board of some sort for writing down key points or for doing direct instruction, and a teacher's desk either in the back or the front of the room. But this kind of typical set up doesn't provide a child with an opportunity to consider experimentation, tinkering, collaborative processes and flexibility. In a 2012 report by Evan Sinar, Richard Wellins and Chris Pacione, fostering innovation effectively requires four main components:

- Inspiring curiosity
- Challenging current perspectives
- Creating freedom and
- Driving discipline

When creating a learning space to support a STEAM approach, it is important to consider how the space is providing students with the opportunity to engage in these critical components. One suggestion is through a Studio/Lab design.

The Studio/Lab design is a flexible learning space arrangement that provides students with the ability to be introduced to, use and create with the strategies that have been taught throughout instruction. There are two components to this design: the studio and the lab and they are distinctly different. The studio is meant to be used as a way to discover and explore the process of learning, while the lab is meant to be the place where that learning is analyzed, evaluated and refined.

The Studio

In an artist's studio, the artist is allowed to play with their tools and experiment broadly and without restriction. There is a strong element of trust that what happens in the studio is an outgrowth of the discovery process for the artist. If the artist is a performer, the studio is a place where they can work alongside their peers, growing in both their own individual abilities and behaviors and learning how to use these cohesively in a larger group for a collective purpose.

For inspiration, go to a local dance studio or look online at artist and musician studios and pay close attention to how they are organized. Most are open spaces without chairs or other distractions. The focus is on the tools and the artists themselves. For instance, a dance studio will have a barre available for stretching and a music studio may have a piano or a group of instruments. An visual artist's studio may have an easel or a potter's wheel, and a graphic artist's studio will have a computer. Most studios have a mirror so that the artist can critique their own work on a continual basis. The rest of what may be present is meant to inspire the artist in some way or to evoke their artistic process. There is nothing extraneous in a studio environment.

Likewise, the classroom studio should be more open and conducive to group practice and reflection. This may mean pushing desks aside to the recesses of the room. Encourage students to think of the learning space as a way to experiment with their strategies and use all of their tools in order to create a new understanding and product that is reflective of their current knowledge. Provide them with inspiration that evokes this kind of experiment using essential questions that require them to think and react deeply to a topic. As practical, attach a time limit to the studio. In the real world of artists, studio time with a coach or instructor is limited and can be expensive, so you make the most of every moment. There is a constant struggle for artists between living completely in the art and being able to move that art into a practical reality. This struggle should exist for your students as well. During studio time, make sure students have a purpose for what they want to accomplish during the studio to move their ideas closer to a transformative output. But, be flexible and open to inspiration since an exploration of one pathway may only lead to a dead end, while another may propel the work forward.

Using a studio atmosphere and culture doesn't need to be complex. Start with simply using the name "studio" when students enter your room. This powerful word will give a totally different context for the work you're about to embark on as a teaching and learning team. Then, create an open space that allows for experimentation as a launchpad for innovation to bubble up to the surface. Try a few of these suggestions to get started:

- Start with a question of the hour and ask students to find ways to explore that topic using the tools found in the studio.

- Practice one or more of the strategies described earlier in this book.

- Use the studio as an idea generator. Have students work in collaborative teams that are organized by their different strengths to think through a problem or to analyze a piece of work.

- Provide a prompt, which could include a piece of artwork, an advertisement, a piece of data, a current event in the school, or a piece of music to develop a response to its core message.

The Lab

The lab environment is a space that takes the creativity and raw ideas garnered through the studio and puts them up for analysis. This is where students can test their theories and ideas, document their findings, evaluate the outcomes and refine their approach. Going through the lab environment may lead to more time in the studio, but it could also mean devising a simple adjustment and going back through the lab process. A lab is a more controlled area than a studio and while they share some similarities, there are also some distinct elements to the lab that do not exist in an artist's studio.

In a lab culture, every tool has a purpose and a place. This is similar to the artist's studio in that there are no extraneous tools lying around the room. However, the use of each tool in the lab is very specific, whereas in the studio the tools themselves are meant to be manipulated and used more freely in creation. A lab is a place where experimentation happens, but this experimentation is defined in a sequence of if/then hypotheses and statements from the start of the process. In the studio, the if/then hypotheses and statements are developed throughout the process, rather than defined right from the beginning. And, while students engage in reflective practice in the studio, the lab space provides them with a way to document those reflections and use them to guide next steps and continue the forward movement of design and implementation.

The classroom lab space, therefore, can be used as a conduit for turning the questions explored in the studio into practical and transformative solutions. This kind of space requires more structure while still maintaining the ability to perform the experiments with fidelity. This means that the space should contain a setup that both fosters sequential processes and yields a valid and reliable output. Some examples of this kind of lab space could include:

- Lab tables or desks organized as longer tables required for some experiments

- Workstations and dedicated zones for each phase of the experiments

- Areas dedicated for research and development

- A common area where groups can gather together for presentations of their findings and experiences

- Organized storage areas for equipment or other "tools" that may be necessary for the work

Once you have determined the layout of your Lab space, then it simply becomes a matter of moving the classroom around to accommodate this need. Students can do this with you and the time it takes to transform the space from studio to lab doesn't need to be overwhelming. Once students know the layout, they can quickly help to create the Lab space or move it back to the Studio space setup. Again, empower the students as much as possible to create the space for their own learning. The Organisation for Economic Co-operation and Development agrees, concluding in their research that successful iterations of innovative school environments provide flexibility, student-centeredness and provisions for transformable learning spaces like the ones provided in this section.

Determining which space to use for a STEAM lesson or approach is dependent upon the focus of the standard and the end result that is intended within the topic being addressed. The Lab could be used to test ideas generated during a studio time, as a way to present findings, research or evidence that would move a project forward, or as a direct instructional pathway. Additionally, the Studio and the Lab could be used in conjunction with one another. Perhaps your classroom has a common area that serves as the studio and surrounding the studio is the lab where instruction is more guided and sequential. As we have seen in the case studies presented here, this will look different in each and every school because it has to work for your students. However, understanding these ideas of space design may help you in the journey towards creating the optimal learning space for this approach in your school.

Classroom vs. Whole-School

How you utilize the STEAM approach is going to be dependent upon your school or district's mission and vision. Many of you may be looking to create a whole-school approach to using STEAM while others may be looking for a way to utilize this in their classrooms because their school is not yet ready to move in this direction. Many of the same principles that were just discussed in designing a space where STEAM can flourish in the classroom can also apply to an entire school. The key to this is in recognizing how these design elements can be used on a larger scale as part of the fabric of the STEAM approach to support each classroom.

First, schools must recognize that this approach is grown organically through careful fostering and pruning over time. Just as we are encouraging students to experiment with seeking out problems and working through solutions, we must model that when implementing this approach throughout the whole school. Not all staff will be on board at first and this is actually desirable. In order for a STEAM approach to spread its roots, it only needs a few seeds to be planted. As with any new initiative, there will be bumps along the way and if you have just a few strong supportive teachers on board, they will be willing to work through that with you and become mentors for others who will undoubtedly go through similar challenges. By starting slowly and with just a few individuals, the approach has the chance to be tended and flourish based upon your own needs as a school community, without being strangled by naysayers.

Second, start with a clear end in mind. Using this, develop one or two practices that will move the needle to that outcome. Model how you would like students to use the STEAM approach. Reconfigure the faculty lounge area or the conference rooms to better foster collaboration and creative thinking. Think about how you are using the space in your building and what might happen if those spaces were redesigned for studio and lab environments. Implement a core problem-solving practice model that could be used in all classrooms for a variety of purposes. This gives everyone a common language right from the beginning to be utilized for any project, lesson, or program that might be developed.

Finally, don't be afraid to cut pieces that are not working. There are always going to be dead branches or flowers that don't bloom. In order for a fresh, healthy outgrowth to take its place, you must prune back the areas of the plant that are no longer servicing the approach. This means that if you try an idea or a project and it doesn't work for your students, then it is okay to stop doing that in replacement with a different idea or project. However, do this with caution. Just as you wouldn't sheer off all of the flowers on the plant, you don't want to cut initiatives that simply haven't been given the proper nourishment or tending. Be sure that you work through what isn't working, why it's not working and what could be done to improve or replace that component in your larger plan towards a STEAM approach school-wide. Always look at all of the data and find the root causes of a perceived failure before labeling it as such; it may just be the discomfort of change that is masking itself as failure.

Templates Don't Exist

There is no cookie-cutter design for implementing a STEAM approach that will work for everyone. The templates for building a STEAM initiative in a school or classroom don't exist because this approach is entirely dependent upon the unique culture of your school community. That doesn't mean, however, that there aren't a few guiding components that all schools or classrooms that use a STEAM approach share in common. These elements act as the loom which holds the approach to a level of integrity in its formation, allowing you to have an infinite number of school-based designs for implementation at your disposal.

Exploration is Everywhere

The invitation to explore and discover is provided to students everywhere in a school or classroom. These could be galleries on the walls, exhibits in unexpected places, or rotating pondering questions that are hung throughout the hallways on the ceilings. Look around the school and provide ways that students can explore "why" to anything that is a part of your building - from the location of the restrooms to the multiple uses of a cafetorium. Encourage students to be inspired and driven by their own curiosity.

Learning is not bottled in a classroom

This is the largest step anyone can take in the STEAM approach, but it is also the most difficult. We want students to be lifelong learners, and yet we model that learning only takes place in a classroom setting. Instead, find ways to bring learning outside of the classroom and through all areas of the school day. Use lunchtime as an opportunity for students to become hands-on learners about food nutrition and culinary skills. Use the arrival and dismissal transportation schedule and structure to explore safety and civil engineering. Actively seek out experiences that bring learning to life in every aspect of the school day.

Collaborative Planning and Intentional Alignments

True STEAM cannot happen without purposeful and natural alignments between standards which are taught in and through two or more content areas and assessed equitably. STEAM initiatives that are successful provide direct collaborative planning time and professional development to support teachers in learning how to find and implement these alignments with integrity. This planning can be shaped in a variety of ways - from weekly or monthly collaborative planning to quarterly long-range planning - but it must be included purposefully from the start.

Assessments are Aligned and Authentic

In order to measure student growth with fidelity, the assessments that are used in a STEAM approach must align with the cognitive demand presented by both standards and must be an authentic representation of individual student learning. If a standard is requiring students to demonstrate their knowledge or skills, then the assessment should provide students with the opportunity to share that demonstration. Additionally, schools may consider developing an assessment profile wherein a variety of different assessments are used to provide a more accurate understanding of student learning. This could include a range of percentages in each selected assessment to ensure a focus is placed on assessments that are more congruent with a growth approach. For instance, schools may explore an assessment profile that consists of 40-50% formative assessments, 30-40% performance assessments and 10-30% summative assessments. This way, there is a shift in the use of and purpose behind the assessments that are being given.

Chapter Review

Throughout this chapter, we have discovered the need for innovative, flexible learning spaces that provide a context for the STEAM-based approach. Designing an environment that provides students with the freedom to create and challenge current perspectives, inspire curiosity and risk-taking, and which still requires a disciplined state of mind is a necessary component to successfully bringing STEAM to life. Before moving on, take a moment to explore the questions in more detail:

1. How would you design your space or school to capture the four keys to an innovative environment for learning?

2. What obstacles do you anticipate in transforming your space to accommodate the kind of flexibility that is required for STEAM?

3. What about a STEAM-designed learning space excites you and inspires your own curiosity?

4. What differences do you see in the development of a STEAM environment for your classroom compared to the development of a STEAM environment for your school?

chapter 7 | there's art in everything

case study #3

Walter Bracken Magnet STEAM Academy

Location: Las Vegas, Nevada

Profile:
- •562 students in grades PreK-5
- •56% receive Free and Reduced Meals
- •Average class size is 26 students
- •Title I Magnet School
- •2013 National Blue Ribbon School
- •Student demographics include 18% Caucasian, 10% Black, 55% Hispanic, 8% Asian, 1% Hawaiian/Pacific Islander, 8% other, and 42% ELL
- •Community: Urban

STEAM Initiative Leaders:
Katie Decker (Principal), Christine Herbert (Theme Coordinator)

Timeframe:
2013-2014 is the 13th year as a STEM/STEAM Magnet

Imagine a place where you could grow your own food, sell it at a farmer's market and invest your profits back into the program or into your own savings account. Or, imagine creating a team to design a musical production that includes sound engineers, tech crews, makeup engineers and marketers. How about developing a class based upon a passion that you have and then creating your own marketing campaign to advertise it to students? If this sounds like fun, that's because it is and the students at Walter Bracken STEAM Academy are proof that play = success.

Katie Decker is a tireless advocate for the success of her students as the principal of Walter Bracken. The high standards that she expects are met on a daily basis, and are the result of a clear vision for bringing vigorous learning experiences throughout the school. She is constantly working to build partnerships with community organizations, parents, businesses and other schools to move this vision forward, while simultaneously supporting, pushing and praising her staff for their integration efforts. When you listen to her speak, she's like the Energizer Bunny...she keeps going and going and going. She is a tenacious force for bringing the art of teaching and learning back to schools. But then again, she didn't have a choice.

Thirteen years ago, Walter Bracken was one of the lowest performing schools in Nevada. Their math proficiency scores stood at just 5.6%. When Katie came on board, the school had just received an MSAP (Magnet Schools Assistance Program) grant to transform itself into a STEM Magnet. The grant was written prior to Katie and her staff coming on board, so at first the vision was being driven by what had been written in the grant. And while, as a faculty they learned quite a bit about what it meant to be a Magnet and what STEM could look like, Katie couldn't shake the feeling that something was missing.

"We were successful with STEM and our kids were improving. We were gaining ground each year and some of the strategies really propelled us forward. But then, we went to the Boston Science Museum and sat through a session with IDEO where we learned about how companies develop teams for creating new solutions and who those people are that sit on those teams. There were scientists and marketers and designers and artists. And it suddenly hit us that school is not preparing our students for ALL of the kinds of jobs that are available," Katie explained. This was a true turning point for Katie and her staff and one more piece of the puzzle slipped into place.

"Then, we saw Georgette Yakman present at an ITEEA conference and realized what was missing for our school was the true intention of engineering and the arts. Once we saw that presentation, we knew that we needed to make the switch. STEAM just makes sense. There's art in everything," proclaimed Katie when I asked her why they moved from STEM to STEAM. She shared that rebranding the school was a struggle at first because STEAM is a relatively new endeavor and others were worried that this was just inserting one more letter into an established acronym in order to bring attention to the arts. Katie didn't let off the gas; she was determined to showcase to her supervisors the thread between engineering and the arts, and how this could be leveraged to propel their school to the next level.

Katie and her team began to reimagine how their school could look and function. At the time, there was a program in place in their district that provided bonus funding if the school took responsibility for their own scores. This Empowerment Program also allowed for a great deal of flexibility in staffing, resources, and schedules but the tradeoff was that the school was held completely accountable for itself. Katie had taken the deal earlier to help move the STEM initiative in the right direction and now she knew what could be done if they kept this same philosophy of accountability and flexibility in place for STEAM. She asked her team to think about the results they were currently getting using STEM and how to make those results better, now that the empowerment money was running out.

What happened next set Walter Bracken on their current pathway to success. The staff explored the concepts of STEAM deeply, made suggestions for classes and experiences through which they could teach their curriculum and how to change the schedule of the school day and year to better accommodate the needs of the students and community. Flexibility with people, time, money and resources remained in place even though there was no bonus. The staff knew that they needed to continue to innovate and re-invent to meet the needs of the students and increase results, not for incentive, but for the kids. There are no excuses at Walter Bracken.

Title I Funds are used to help staff the two computer labs before and after school to ensure that all students can get their homework done on time. Additional funding through a partnership with The Lanni Family Foundation makes the construction of all of the gardens possible. It also provides Walter Bracken with unrestricted monies that they can use to innovate. Because it is a magnet school, the whole community needs to commit to supporting student success, which means that parents are expected to ensure that their students are getting their work done at home so that school can become a place where students play with their new knowledge. Parents are happy to do their part, as evidenced by the 1,000 applications for 100 spots received each year. These parents commit because they are confident in the results.

Remember that dismal 5.6% math proficiency rating when Walter Bracken started down this road 13 years ago? Currently, the school average proficiency rate in math is 90%. That's 20% higher than the district average of 70% and 19% higher than the state's 71% math proficiency scores. And it's not just in math. Science proficiency is at 91%, compared to the district's 54% and the state's 55% average. And in reading, the school has an 86% proficiency, while the district maintains a 59% and the state averages a 61% proficiency score. Obviously, these kind of numbers are impressive, but that's not what drives Katie and her staff.

"We're closing the gaps; we're doing it. If you do high-quality teaching, the rest will be fine. If you focus on test scores, you'll lose," states Katie as she eagerly moves the conversation to the ways that they ARE doing it - in all areas. Here's a glimpse into some of the ways this school is bringing STEAM to all facets of instruction:

Structure

Students receive direct instruction in Math, Language Arts, Science and Social Studies, as well as Music, Art, Physical Education and Media. However, integrated instruction is highly valued and expected whenever possible. Using the philosophy of project-based learning through the STEAM approach has proven to be a successful method of implementation for the students at Walter Bracken. Therefore, a flipped model of instruction is utilized whenever possible. Students receive homework using a variety of open sources online to gather knowledge about multiple topics. Each content area has a webpage with dedicated apps and online resources that students can access for instructional support. When students come to school, they are expected to use what they learned at home and apply it to projects and lessons developed which encourage discovery and creation across content areas.

There are several lab areas available to students, including a math lab, Lego room, physical science lab and a life science lab. Additionally, there is a greenhouse, multiple raised beds that are used by all classes for growing fresh herbs and vegetables, saltwater and freshwater aquarium exhibits, a tortoise habitat and a student-run bank called the "Piggy Bank." This bank allows students to learn the values of saving by providing them with a way to deposit their money into a dedicated bank account. No withdraws are permitted. Volunteers from a variety of local business partners run the bank by collecting deposits while students are responsible for maintaining their own bank book to keep track of their savings. When the bank's customers leave the school, they receive a check for the whole amount they deposited in their tenure at the school.

Additionally, the school has a life-size chess board outside for students to practice their critical-thinking and strategy skills. The walls around the school are covered with large infographics of math and science processes and skills, as well music keyboards that identify the names of the notes and their solfege equivalent. The goal is to provide an environment where students are surrounded by the wonderment of their world. The flexibility, surrounded by a framework of responsibility, is what allows this kind of structure to work for the school.

Creating Buy-In

What is taught at Walter Bracken is similar to what is taught in other schools around the country. They have all of the standard courses, and even use some of the same best practices for realities you can't (and shouldn't) escape. For instance, students still need to know their math facts because without them, they will be at a loss when those skills are needed for a later application. So Rocket Math, a web-based resource from the Otter Creek Institute, is used to help students master the math facts of addition, subtraction, multiplication and division. Additionally, this allows students to take short bursts of online tests in the program that provide teachers with data on their progress using the direct instruction.

Reading is taught through a choice-based, series-based approach. All support staff members have a reading series in their room. Students can shop for a reading-level appropriate series online at the school's web database and find which staff members has that series in their location. Students then go to that staff member and request a copy of each book in the series as they progress. Once they complete the series, they receive a charm to add to their reading charm necklace throughout the school year. What the staff has noticed is a high-level of student engagement through discussions with their peers about the series as they progress. Nancy Drew, the Hardy Boys and Grimm's Fairytales have all made a resurgence in their building. Plus, the students are strengthening their relationships with a variety of staff members, further cementing the fact that the success of each child is built upon the investment of all school staff members.

But perhaps the hallmark of the instruction that is in place for Walter Bracken lies within its positive incentives programs. The Junior Chef program gives students the chance to experience first-hand the art of culinary practice. The school invites various chefs to come in and share cooking techniques with students, how to craft a healthy plate and uses the food that students grow in their own raised beds outside of their classrooms. In the very near future, students will use hydroponics to supplement their own lunch program. The school plans to have their students design the space and engage their high school feeder students to engineer it and transform the design into a reality.

The school also employs the use of Exploration Classes in its instructional design for learning. These are STEAM-based classes of choice that are offered during the last hour of the day, twice a week, three times per year. The classes are unique in that they are choice-based for both teachers and students. Teachers are given the opportunity to teach something that they are passionate about and are responsible for designing a course around the topic. Not only that, but they must then market the class to the students who are then able to choose which three courses they would like to participate in for the year. Teachers must make the course enticing because if there are not enough students that sign up for a course, they must teach another section of choice that was more popular. The school also makes an effort to survey students to find out what they would be interested in so that teachers can match their interests with those of the students. Instruction is truly a collaborative effort between teachers and students throughout this process.

Community Partners

Finally, this kind of flexibility, engagement, and hands-on learning would not be possible without a strong level of support from the community. Much of that is because Katie pounds the pavement to ask organizations directly for their help. Currently, Walter Bracken partners with the United Way, Young Philanthropy Society, Andson, Junior Achievement and Silver State Credit Union for their Piggy Bank project, and Leadership Las Vegas and the Las Vegas Rotary support the school in its fundraising efforts as well as sponsoring events and providing additional materials that are needed along the way. High school students are working with teachers in writing integrated lessons and visiting the school to lead students through these plans. And, not only do chefs come out monthly to participate in leading the Junior Chefs program, but local artisans and teaching artists are also regular partners in creating, implementing, and sharing arts-integrated lessons and projects.

Katie advises that other schools who are looking to bring experiential learning opportunities to their students be just as purposeful and tenacious in their approach to partners as they are in instructional development and support. "It's important to be constantly communicating with these organizations and asking for what you need," she emphasizes and goes on to recommend that you are as specific as possible when approaching others to support your school initiative. "Organizations want to help, but they need to know exactly what you need and how they can be of service to you," Katie shares. Schools may want to consider creating a list of their needs and a list of organizations and partners in the surrounding area. Then, try looking for direct matches between both lists to find the ways you can build sustainable partnering relationships.

Opportunities and Obstacles

While this is an impressive and comprehensive example for building and using the STEAM approach, there were significant challenges to overcome in order to get to this point. The biggest hurdle that faced Walter Bracken is in the communication of a clear and consistent vision. When they started down this pathway, the school was following the vision of a grant that was designed by someone who was not a part of their team. This put them in a position of following something in which they didn't have a stake or claim to its success. So when the focus shifted from STEM to STEAM, Katie knew that she needed to build the vision collaboratively and to communicate it over and over again.

But to build that vision, they needed a place to start. With so many possibilities, where do you begin? This kind of open-endedness is almost paralyzing to a group. So, they decided to look at data and use this as the compelling need for change. Once they found the need for change, they could then begin to share ideas for how to accomplish the change, using data-driven decisions. This was the key to unlocking a vision that supported a mission of providing students with a high-quality education through investigative experiences. If they were going to talk the talk, they needed to walk the walk.

"We let people's passion and opinion drive decisions rather than facts and data," shares Katie and goes further by explaining that in her school, people are encouraged to support their divergent opinions based upon evidence. What has worked for her has been to deliver the message and idea directly to staff and then speak with each member one on one. It's important to take the time to do this so that you can understand all of the barriers. And if someone has a barrier or disagrees, it's important to remember that it's just one person. Just because their voice is louder than the group doesn't mean it's the consensus of the group. When you hear disagreements about the approach or idea, then encourage those individuals to dig a bit deeper and provide evidence to support their opinion. Survey students, do a little research and bring back the results. Find out if there is validity to that position and then discuss it.

The final step in the process that Katie outlines for obstacles along the way is to conduct a vote. Everyone needs to be invested and their voices need to carry weight, so a vote provides them with that opportunity. Of course, by doing the legwork ahead of time into understanding and working through the barriers, the result of that vote should already be a foregone conclusion, but the success of an idea or initiative lies within that vote. That's because Walter Bracken has a rule: if the group's vote results are different than what an individual supported, the individual needs to act with integrity to get behind the group's decision. If not, then the initiative will fail, as will the efforts to move the students forward. When asked if there were instances where people refused to get behind an idea, Katie shared that there were a few times that this has occurred. But in the end, "people want to see their kids succeed," she said and this fact always trumps personal feelings.

Conclusion

In this final case study, we can see the evolution of what STEAM can become over time and the remarkable results the approach can have upon both students and teachers. One of the highlights of this interview for me was to see both the horizontal alignment and consistency of the approach across the school and the vertical alignment that is shown by working with the feeder schools to ensure that the tenets of STEAM are being embraced long after students leave Walter Bracken. This school, more than any other highlighted in this book, shows the possibilities for STEAM beyond any grade-level of school and moves the conversation towards creating learning opportunities that are fully immersive and designed to create a place for play. What's the secret sauce of this kind of success? As Katie Decker so beautifully concludes, it's "everybody working together to make a magical learning experience" for each and every child. It's about time we all created some magic.

chapter 8 | cycle of curricular development

When you walk into Ed's apartment at the local assisted living home, the first thing you notice is that everything has a specific place and there is nothing out of order. The books are all shelved, the picture frames have been freshly polished, and the floor has been recently vacuumed. The space is small, but not cramped, and the furniture that was kept after downsizing from his home of 60 years is comfortably arranged to maximize the features of the apartment. On the walls, there hang a few generic pieces of artwork and photographs of his three children, many grandchildren and great-grandchildren. But pride of place among his memories hang the framed puzzles that he completed over the decades with his precious wife, whom he lost only three years earlier.

These puzzles create pictures of everything from historical events to animals in the fields. The finished picture didn't matter so much as the challenge presented by the puzzle itself. Ed doesn't work on puzzles that have less than 1,000 pieces. In fact, his preference is to work on puzzles with 5,000 or more pieces because he finds that the process of putting them together keeps his mind sharp and his spirit hungry with anticipation, curiosity and eventually triumph as he places the last piece in its perfect home. When asked how he even knew where to start working through such a complex and overwhelming process, he replied, "oh, you know. I do what everyone else does. I start with the corners. You've got to start with the corners so you can begin to create your frame. Everything else is just a matter of time, patience and hard work!"

Working through the integration process of the STEAM approach is exactly like putting together those puzzles that Ed enjoys so much. The process appears to be a Herculean task when looking at all of the pieces that are required, but choosing to start with the corners and building the framework will ensure that through time, patience and hard work, STEAM will eventually become a way of life in your classroom or school.

The Four Corners

The corner pieces have already been identified through the previous chapters in this book. The first corner is about defining and understanding what STEAM is and how it can be used with integrity. The second corner provides teachers with specific strategies, tools and resources which help to service a STEAM lesson or unit of study. The third corner includes specific behaviors that are necessary to assist in propelling the STEAM process and leveraging these behaviors for the success of all students. The final corner addresses the importance of how learning spaces are arranged and intentionally created to allow for the STEAM process to occur. Now you have unpacked each of these four corners individually, it's time to create a frame that connects these corners together for a cohesive approach to teaching and learning.

The Frame: An Integrated Curricular Model

To be clear, STEAM is not a curriculum. STEAM is an approach. This important distinction must be made because too often when developing a model for change, schools try to create or buy curriculum to "fix" the problem. STEAM is not a singular curricular area; it is an approach to connecting and deepening each of the curricular areas that it addresses: science, technology, engineering, the arts and mathematics. Each of these individual areas DO have a curriculum which must be taught and assessed through the standards that have been provided.

That being said, what the STEAM approach does allow us to do in a curriculum is embed its practices through an integrated curricular model. Meaning that we can use the STEAM approach with the specific purpose of connecting curriculum through specific units or lessons of study that embed high-leverage strategies and which fully require a shift in the behaviors and learning environments to support student achievement of the identified standards. To break that complex statement apart, take a look at the model below:

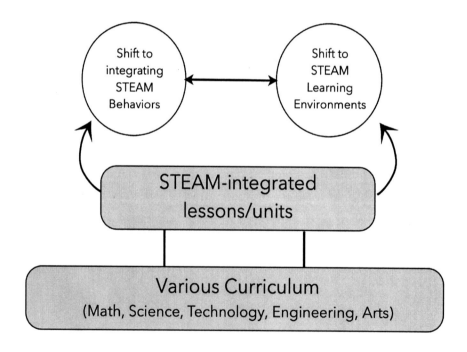

The cycle of an integrated curricular model can be used for a single lesson or unit (as shared in chapter 1) or an entire scope and sequence of integrating multiple content areas, which is the purpose of this chapter. Keep in mind, however, that the curriculum for each area is still a separate entity that is taught and assessed for its own distinct standards. What an integrated curricular model does is to provide concentrated touchpoint areas where specific curricula can be aligned, taught and assessed together for a greater impact.

Step 1: Create a Collaborative Team

You'll need to identify areas across the curriculum that could naturally be aligned through the STEAM approach. This requires more than just one set of eyes. Everyone has a lens through which they look at curriculum, generally based upon their own experiences. Therefore, a collaborative team of educators or specialists from each of the STEAM content areas is recommended to begin this work. In the middle and high school grade bands, this may look like a team of educators from the science, technology, engineering, arts and mathematics departments or classes (many schools do not have an engineering or technology department). At the elementary level where educators are more generalized in the teaching practices, choose a team that includes educators with strong backgrounds or interests in the science, technology, engineering and math curriculum areas, as well as all of the fine arts educators. Each fine arts educator will bring a different understanding and specific knowledge of an art form and it's important to capture these similarities and differences.

The work of this collaborative team will be to bring their curriculum together and begin to look for places of congruence and alignment, as well as gaps that exist in their current curriculum that could be filled through intentional STEAM lessons or units of study. This team will need to meet on a regular basis and have a clear process in their approach to identifying, aligning and creating STEAM-integrated touch points. This can be done per grade level through individual standards, grade bands (i.e.: K-2, 3-5, 6-8) through Anchor standards and processes, or through individual courses. Think about not only the horizontal benefits of creating integrated touch points for learning across a grade level or subject area, but also in the vertical benefits of choosing touch points that are aligned K-5, K-8 or K-12. This will guide the structure of the collaborative process for this team.

Step 2: Identify the Gaps

Once your team is gathered and a vision for the process is identified, then it's time to begin digging deeply into each of the curricula represented. As a team, begin to identify areas that are similar across the content area curricula, and those that are obviously different. Discuss the purpose behind each of these elements and how they serve the intention of the curriculum. For instance, if the science curriculum contains a vertical alignment that identifies what was done prior to each lesson and what will be done after each lesson, but the music curriculum does not contain this element, address why it's important to include or not to include this element. These discussions will provide each member of the team with critical context surrounding the content, as well as provide prompts for further investigations.

Additionally, use this time to identify areas where students struggle in a course and discuss what may be missing from the curriculum which could be a root cause. These areas of struggle are the perfect opportunity to insert a STEAM-integrated lesson or unit and are a good place to start in what can be an overwhelming amount of material to cover. What the team will begin to notice is that dedicated STEAM lessons or units can be used strategically to enhance and deepen the learning experience through the curriculum.

Step 3: Use Essential Questions for Inquiry

Once the gaps across and within the various curricula have been identified and opportunities for STEAM-developed lessons or units have been selected, the team must then look at the content standards addressed in that curriculum and develop an essential question that is aligned to the expectation of that standard. This essential question will allow the team to identify a naturally aligned content standard from another content area to which the essential question also applies. For example, if my math essential question is "How can I use fractions?" I could use this same essential question in music for note values and time signatures, or in visual arts for proportion. This could then lead to the identification of specific standards in both math and the arts area which will guide the development of a STEAM lesson or unit.

The team should also identify pathways for inquiry based upon the essential questions that have been developed. This way, there are multiple avenues and choices for students to explore, discover, and create using STEAM-based practices and skills. These inquiry pathways begin to narrow the lesson or unit focus and can also serve as connective branches for other content areas or additional study within the curriculum.

Step 4: Schema-Based Curriculum Mapping

The development of the essential questions will naturally lead to a schema-based curriculum map as an outgrowth of the integrated planning process. Once essential questions have been created, these can be used as topic area foci. The team can place the essential question in the center of the document and identify all of the ways that could be used to explore, discover and create surrounding that question. Thus, in our previous example of "How can I use fractions?" a schema map could be created with this question at the center, followed by not only how music and art address that question, but also science, technology, engineering, dance, and theatre. For each large content area identified that also explores the essential question, the next step is to articulate the context by which those curricular areas delve into that inquiry. In music, it may be through note values and time signature, while in theatre it may through the use of scenery in proportion to the actors and the stage. Once the context has been stated for each area, then the standards which address that context can be identified. This is also an opportunity for connections across content areas and between contexts to be brought to the surface and extrapolated for additional study.

Once fully-formed schema maps have been developed based upon the essential questions for each curriculum area, then curriculum maps can begin to be created. These maps will have the essential questions provided as the focus for lesson or unit creation, supported by the identified aligned standards from two or more content areas. Skills and/or processes that students may need in order to achieve those standards should also be identified, as well as how those standards can be assessed equitably. Finally, a sample lesson idea of just 2-3 sentences can be supplied as a prompt for larger lesson development. These curriculum maps provide all educators in the school or district with the ability to design lessons that meet the integrity of a STEAM approach to teaching and learning, while still maintaining respect for their abilities as a creative and knowledgeable practitioner to create a lesson that meets the needs of their own students.

Step 5: Weaving Strategies into Integrated Instruction

This brings us to a key question: should the integrated curricular team create STEAM lesson plans? The answer will depend upon the needs of your staff and students, as well as the capacity of the educators that are a part of the collaborative team. Certainly, no one wants to take away an individual teacher's creative freedom. Some would argue that by providing specific STEAM integrated lessons for teachers, it will strip away their ability to modify instruction based on the needs of their students. On the other hand, providing model lessons for teachers to use can ease their anxiety about creating integrated lessons on their own with limited support or guidance. Additionally, these model lessons may act as a sample that teachers can then refer to in the development of their own STEAM lessons.

With limited professional development time and resources available to teachers, I am of the opinion that we should provide our educators with built-in supports for an approach like STEAM throughout their curricula. This includes providing them with sample lesson plans, assessments and strategies to support this instructional model. We can't stop at providing teachers with maps without their understanding of how those maps translate into a full-developed lesson. We wouldn't model that practice for our students and we shouldn't model it for our teachers. Everyone needs an example of what a high-quality, vigorous and meaningful integrated lesson should contain. However, we must also provide our educators with an understanding that this is simply a model and that they should use it as a springboard for their own STEAM lessons.

In a curriculum that contains STEAM-integrated touch points, ideally there would be a schema-based curriculum map at the beginning of the curricular document which is referenced at each touchpoint. Each touchpoint area would contain a fully-developed lesson, as well as an aligned assessment, with an explanation on the process and purpose behind the lesson design. Additionally, since each essential question developed produced a schema map with multiple ways to address that question, refer back to this map and highlight the many different ways a teacher could approach these standards. This way, teachers are provided with a supportive model of instruction that also gives them the power of choice to develop their own lesson to address the selected content standards based within their individual strengths and weaknesses and which meets the complexities of their classroom.

Another way to support teachers in STEAM-integrated instruction and provide consistency throughout all curriculum areas is through weaving selected strategies into instruction through the lesson plans and curriculum scope and sequence. Choose strategies that can be used across disciplines in a variety of settings and include them in the curriculum documents. Provide the steps for using the strategies and weave them into each discipline at multiple times throughout the curriculum. This way, the strategies are being used with fidelity, and students can experience them in different ways across their school day. For instance, if you choose to use the iNotice3 strategy, you could embed this into the science, math, and arts curriculum at various times throughout the scope and sequence of the year. The strategy remains the same, but because it is used in multiple ways, students can begin to leverage it as connective tool for exploration and problem-solving across areas.

Step 6: Reflection and Feedback

It is important that we provide educators with multiple opportunities for reflection and to provide feedback. Too often, our teachers are so busy with all of the tasks they need to accomplish that they are not able to take time to think about what is working and what may need to be refined. By including reflective thinking prompts within our curricula, we are bringing that reflection process to the foreground of instruction. When possible, try to bring reflection to life throughout the school day. Pose questions in the faculty lounge, send out a tweet or email a prompt to teachers to think about throughout the day and to share their thoughts at a faculty meeting or morning coffee time. We all get better when we have the chance to deeply reflect and share our own struggles and triumphs along the way.

In the development of an integrated curricular model of instruction, be sure to include reflection prompts that can cross content areas. As with weaving strategies across disciplines, embedding reflections that can be discussed between teachers no matter what their content area is important for consistency and as a way to make the self-reflection process visible. When you can share a struggle or a triumph with someone who doesn't teach what you teach but who still understands it because they are going through the same thing, it makes teaching and learning a collaborative effort.

And don't just stop at reflective opportunities built into the curriculum for teachers. Also be sure to include reflection opportunities for students, as well as tangible ways that they can provide feedback about a lesson, unit or selected approach. Remember the Talk Back circles that Melanie Skankey used at North Elementary? These are a critical piece to her use of integration because students are able to express and take ownership of their individual learning process, as well as how their journey impacts and influences the group as a whole. Plus, educators are able to hear how a student is processing and investing in their own learning and can discover valuable insights into the needs of each of their students.

In both teacher and student reflection opportunities, there must be a way to collect feedback based within those reflections. Whether that be through a survey, a comment dropbox or a collaborative discussion, feedback must be collected and used to make the process better. There is nothing worse than soliciting feedback from others and then doing nothing with the results. That is the quickest way to lose trust from others. Instead, remember that this is a cycle. Be transparent with the feedback received, share the results and state publicly how those results will be used to better the process. This holds everyone accountable and makes everyone feel valued, while simultaneously making the integration of STEAM even better.

The Rest of the Puzzle

Now that the framework is complete, you're done, right? Well, not quite. After all, there is a whole puzzle that needs to be finished. Just because you have the frame in place doesn't mean that the picture is clear. There will still be a lot of fuzziness surrounding how you use STEAM in your classroom or school. You will need to try out pieces in different places, you will need to be strategic as you work through one piece at a time, and you will become frustrated and may need to walk away to get your vision back. But always come back. As Ed reminded us at the start of this chapter: the whole puzzle takes time, patience and hard work to accomplish. The STEAM approach is no different and we should all go into it with this kind of expectation.

I asked Ed if he ever gave up on a puzzle. "Oh yes, plenty of times," he replied as he rocked back and forth in his recliner, staring fondly at one of the framed jigsaws on the wall. "But I couldn't let it go for long. The thing just kept gnawing at me because I knew that it could be done. I just needed a minute to let my eyes rest and my mind clear. The pieces always fall together if you give them a chance," he said as he continued to rock. Back and forth, back and forth.

Final Thoughts

As we move to the conclusion of the narrative part of this book and into the lessons and assessments, I want to take a moment to tie up some loose ends. STEAM is certainly a newer approach in the realm of education, but its foundation lies within a body of evidence surrounding the power of integration through the arts. Our most innovative and successful leaders are artists in their own right. Steve Jobs, Albert Einstein, Jack Andraka, Temple Grandin, Eesah Khare and the thousands of other inventors, scientists, technology developers, and mathematicians are all artists in some capacity. So it only makes sense that we not only include, but intentionally study and apply the skills and principles behind the arts in and through our instruction. It's not enough to find and analyze a problem. We must have the capacity to use what we know to create what has not yet been invented. The arts are the avenue to making this transition.

As we saw in each of the case studies throughout this book, it takes a passionate leader to bring this approach to life. Hopefully, you can see that the role of leader can be both an administrator and a teacher. Our educators have so much to offer as models and leaders of instruction! If you are a teacher reading this, I hope that you recognize that kernel of truth about yourself: you can be the leader of this change in your classroom, school or district. As you move forward and your students are successful, others will notice what you are doing and want to be a part of the change. You have all the power you need to make this approach work for your students. If you're an administrator, my hope is that you are inspired by the school-level leaders in these case studies as the visionaries that they are in 21st century schools. These leaders understand their roles as facilitators and collaborators with all stakeholders, and simply remove the barriers in whatever form they exist. You are most certainly overburdened and frustrated by the expectations placed on your school or district, and this is definitely justified. But if you want to see progress and improvement for all students and teachers, then your job is simple: remain true to the vision of STEAM for your school and provide whatever supports are needed to turn that vision into a reality.

The rest of this book is meant to provide you with samples and models as a baseline for STEAM integrated lessons and units. Use them in whatever way works best for you: as a resource, reference, or collaborative prompt. Whatever you do with them, don't wait around for someone to tell you that it's okay to use these for instruction. Take this moment and commit to engaging ALL students, to bringing creativity and passion back to your profession, and to continually building momentum one step as a time towards teaching and learning that is reflective of the world in which the possibilities have yet to be imagined. No permission required.

part 3 | lessons and assessments

grades | K-2

In this section, you will find fully-developed sample lessons and assessments that incorporate each of the strategies shared in Part 1 of this resource. Each lesson also comes with grade-band extensions to provide some flexibility for you in their use. Please note that each grade-band must address a comparable, grade-level appropriate standard. Remember: these are suggestions to get you started. Feel free to adapt and change as needed for your students.

Part 3 is arranged by grade-level band, followed by art form. In this section, for instance, you will find lessons and assessments for grades K-2, organized by visual arts, drama, music and dance. This will be followed by sections for grades 3-5, 6-8 and finally, 9-12.

VISUAL ARTS

Integrated Lesson Plan | Badge Craft Strategy

Content Area: Math	Fine Arts Area: Visual Arts	Lesson Title:	Stained Glass Shapes
Grade Level: K-2	Duration: (2) 45-60 minute class periods		Teacher:

Standards and Alignment

Content Area Standard(s):	Fine Arts Standard(s):
CCSS.Math.Content.1.G.A.2 Compose two- dimensional shapes to create a composite shape, and compose new shapes from the composite shape.	Visual Art: **Artistic Process**: Responding **Anchor Standard**: Perceive and analyze artistic work.

Big Idea:	Students use analysis of Frank Lloyd Wright's artwork to learn about and compose shapes.	Essential Question:	How are shapes formed?
21st Century Skills:	Creativity, Collaboration, Evaluate Information, Critical Thinking	Key Vocabulary:	Two-dimensional, rectangles, squares, trapezoids, triangles, half circles, quarter circles, shape, line

Vertical Alignment	Before Lesson:	During Lesson:	After Lesson:
	Identifying and manipulating two-dimensional shapes in isolation	Identifying, describing and manipulating two-dimensional shapes as composites.	Decompose created shapes into two and four equal shares.
Materials List:	Pencils, pens, glue sticks, tissue paper, contact paper, scrap paper, Frank Lloyd Wright stained glass window examples, projector, computer		

Instructional Delivery (guided, collaborative, and self-directed)

Student Learning Outcome(s):	I can create new shapes using examples from a famous artist.
Pre-Engagement:	**Pre-assessment:** View a piece of Frank Lloyd Wright's stained glass works together as a class. Have students identify what they see, what they think and what they are curious about within the example. **Engagement:** Have students look specifically at the shapes in the artwork and identify everything they can by name (i.e.: square, rectangle, triangle, etc). **Process:**
Focal Lesson:	Use the Badge Craft strategy to explore these shapes in more detail. At the first station, ask students , as a group, to select one of the shapes they identified and notice how many times that shape repeats within the stained glass example. At the next station, ask students to notice the variations of each of the times that shape appears - length, width, height, color, no color, etc. At the third station ask students to identify how the shape they chose is layered within the stained glass. Is the shape on top of another shape? Are there any layers? Why would the artist choose to do that? What new shape does this create?

Focal Lesson:	When students are finished at each station, have them complete a single badge for their group with each of their station observations written or drawn in the spaces provided. Have them share their badge with the rest of the class and then notice similarities and differences between the shapes that were identified. Ask students: how did the artist create new shapes from the other two-dimensional shapes in the window? Provide students with a piece of contact paper and several pieces of tissue paper in various colors, sizes, and shapes. Ask students to include at least one circle, square and triangle in their work. Using their observations from their badges, students will then create their own stained glass model by cluing their tissue paper onto the contact paper. **Be sure that they design their work on a piece of scrap paper first.**
Integrated Assessment and Extension	**Stained Glass Window** When finished, have students share their stained glass window by describing the shapes they chose and how each of the shapes they chose are different or layered with each other to create a composite shape. Finished products can be assessed through a rubric.

| Integrated Assessment and Extension | **Suggested Grade-Band Extensions**

3-5: Using the same activity, have students study the stained glass window examples by classifying the two-dimensional figures based on the presence or absence of parallel or perpendicular lines or absence of angles caused by the frame holding the shapes in place. Have students create their stained glass windows using these same lines and angles to frame their shapes.

6-8: Students can create the window at scale, based upon a rendered model previously produced.

9-12: Design a stained glass window for a historic home which is also energy and cost efficient. |

Reflection Opportunities

| Student Reflections Prompts: | **Key Questions to Ask Students:**
1.How do you create a new composite shape?
2. How do artists use shapes to communicate? | Teacher Reflection Prompts: | **Key Questions to Ask Yourself:**
1. Was there a seamless connection between the art and math in this lesson?
2. What pieces of this lesson were a challenge? Which pieces were most engaging for me and my students? |

Stained Glass Shapes Formative Assessment Rubric

Content Standard Assessed: **CCSS.Math.Content.1.G.A.2** Compose two-dimensional shapes to create a composite shape, and compose new shapes from the composite shape.

Arts Standards Assessed: Visual Art: **Artistic Process:** Responding **Anchor Standard**: Perceive and analyze artistic work.

FOCAL ASSESSMENT QUESTIONS

Math: Can this student identify and compose with two-dimensional shapes?
Art: Can this student respond to their perception of shape by creating an original piece of artwork in the style of Frank Lloyd Wright?

Math Look-Fors	Art Look-Fors
☐ Student can identify two-dimensional shapes	☐ Student can make multiple observations about a piece of artwork
○ Student can create two-dimensional shapes with accuracy	○ Student can identify and use two-dimensional shapes in their artwork
○ Student can create new shapes from more than one two-dimensional shape	○ Student can apply artistic skill to create multilayered artwork using two-dimensional shapes
○ Student can demonstrate an original idea from a composite of two-dimensional shapes	○ Student can use mixed media to create an original composition

DRAMA

Integrated Lesson Plan	Build-a-Character Strategy

Content Area: Math	Fine Arts Area: Theatre	Lesson Title: Character Shapes

Grade Level: K-2	Duration: (2) 45-60 minute class periods	Teacher:

Standards and Alignment

Content Area Standard(s):	Fine Arts Standard(s):
CCSS.Math.Content.1.G.A.1 Distinguish between defining attributes (e.g, triangles are closed and three-sided) versus non-defining attributes (e.g., color, orientation, overall size); build and draw shapes to possess defining attributes.	Theatre: **Artistic Process:** Creating **Anchor Standard**: Generate and conceptualize artistic ideas and work.

Big Idea:	Shapes contain specific characteristics	Essential Question:	How can we characterize shapes?
21st Century Skills:	Creativity, Collaboration, Evaluate Information, Critical Thinking	Key Vocabulary:	Two-dimensional shapes, three-dimensional shapes, character, energy, facial expression, gesture, related

Vertical Alignment	Before Lesson:	During Lesson:	After Lesson:
	Identifying and classifying objects as either two-dimensional or three-dimensional.	Evaluating, describing and creating relationships between 2-D and 3-D objects.	Creating a composite shape using either 2 or more 2-D shapes or 2 or more 3-D figures.

Materials List:	Examples of 2-dimensional and 3-dimensional figures, open space for movement, paper and pencils, and possibly a computer, microphone and recording software.

Instructional Delivery (guided, collaborative, and self-directed)

Student Learning Outcome(s):	I can create characters of a shape family.

Pre-Engagement:	**Pre-assessment:**
	Review a series of two-dimensional geometric shapes (circles, squares, rectangles, triangles, etc) and ask students to identify the shape, as well as it's defining characteristics (4 lines, 3 lines, curved line, etc).
	Engagement:
	Have students use their bodies to create the shapes they previously identified. Then, have them work in teams to create the same shape together. Ask: How was the process similar and different when you had to work with others to create the shape versus working alone?

Focal Lesson:	Use the Build-a-Character strategy to explore the characteristics of selected 2-D shapes. Invite students to gather into groups of 4-6 people. Provide them with the elements of a character and explore the meaning of each of these elements.
	Then, assign each group a 2-D shape. Ask students to use their actor's hats to create the characteristics for their shape in a frozen image. For instance, if a group was given a circle, they will need to show what a circle's facial expression would look like, what the energy level would be, how it would move, how it's voice may sound, and what one gesture would best capture it as a "circle".
	Each group will present their shape and the audience will provide feedback about the characterizations: Did they make sense? Did it capture that shape? What could you tell me about that shape by watching that performance?
	Now, show students the two-dimensional figures' comparable three-dimensional figures (sphere's, cubes, pyramids, etc) and discuss what is similar and what is different about the 2-D shapes and the 3-D figures. Explore how the third dimension was created.
	Ask students to create their characterizations again, but this time, two groups will need to join together to create 3-D characterizations. The five characteristics requested remain the same, but this time, two groups will need to create the facial expression, energy, movement, voice and gesture for the comparable 3-D figure.
	Each group will present and this time, the audience will compare the 2-D character to the new 3-D character and provide any insights as to what was the same, what was different, and how the group created the new 3-D version.

Integrated Assessment and Extension	**Geometric Shape Family Drama**

Geometric Shape Family Drama

Students will create an opening scene from a play that introduces the audience to the Geometric Shape Family. In small groups, students will collaborate to create a way to introduce each of the following shapes: square, circle, triangle, cube, sphere and pyramid using their previous characterizations. They must also find a way to share with the audience who is related to whom (i.e.: square and cube, circle and sphere, etc) and any distant relatives (rectangles, cylinders, etc). For the youngest students, they can dictate this to an adult or into computer recording software. Other students can write their scripts, and then perform their drama for the class. Use the rubric at the end of this lesson for an assessment.

Suggested Grade-Band Extensions

3-5: Use the same activity, but instead of basic shapes, use lines, points, rays and angles as part of two-dimensional figures. Use the lines, points, rays and angles to develop familial relationships with basic shapes (i.e.: all rectangles have 4 right angles) to create the characterizations.

6-8: Use the creation of the play as the launch pad for finding and solving a real-world problem. During the lesson, provide a word problem that requires students to use facts about supplementary, complementary, vertical and adjacent angles to characterize a solution to the problem. Then, have students create their own word problems based upon the established relationships that must be solved through the creation of the play.

9-12: Utilize cross-sections of three-dimensional objects to model the characterization of the relationship between the two-dimensional and three-dimensional objects.

Reflection Opportunities			
Student Reflections Prompts:	**Key Questions to Ask Students:** 1.What are characteristics of 2-D and 3-D shapes? 2. How are 2-D and 3-D shapes related?	Teacher Reflection Prompts:	**Key Questions to Ask Yourself:** 1. Was there a seamless connection between the theatre and math in this lesson? 2. What pieces of this lesson were a challenge? Which pieces were most engaging for me and my students?

Character Shapes Scene Assessment Rubric

Content Standard Assessed: **CCSS.Math.Content.1.G.A.1** Distinguish between defining attributes (e.g, triangles are closed and three-sided) versus non-defining attributes (e.g., color, orientation, overall size); build and draw shapes to possess defining attributes.

Arts Standards Assessed: Theatre: **Artistic Process:** Creating **Anchor Standard**: Generate and conceptualize artistic ideas and work.

Criteria	Distinguished Level (4)	Excelled Level (3)	Adequate Level (2)	Basic Level (1)
The scene accurately demonstrates the attributes of two-dimensional and three-dimensional objects	All attributes of the two and three-dimensional objects demonstrated in the scene are correct	Most attributes of the two and three-dimensional objects demonstrated in the scene are correct	Some of the attributes of the two and three-dimensional objects demonstrated in the scene are correct	Few to none of the attributes of the two and three-dimensional objects demonstrated in the scene are correct
The scene uses character elements to synthesize the attributes of of two and three dimensional objects	The scene contains all of the assigned characterizations (facial expression, voice, gesture, energy, and movement) and all are appropriate choices for each object	The scene contains most of the assigned characterizations (facial expression, voice, gesture, energy, and movement) and all or most are appropriate choices for each object	The scene contains some of the assigned characterizations (facial expression, voice, gesture, energy, and movement) and some or most are appropriate choices for each object	The scene contains few or none of the assigned characterizations (facial expression, voice, gesture, energy, and movement) and few to none are appropriate choices for each object

The scene accurately defines the relationship between comparable two and three-dimensional objects	The scene provides a clear and obvious definition of the relationship between comparable two and three-dimensional objects	The scene provides a definition of the relationship between comparable two and three-dimensional objects	The scene provides a vague or broad definition of the relationship between comparable two and three-dimensional objects	The scene does not provide a definition of the relationship between comparable two and three-dimensional objects
Students all work together to act out the defining elements of each object introduced	All students in the group have an active role in the creation and performance of the scene.	Most students in the group have an active role in the creation and performance of the scene.	Some students in the group have an active role in the creation and performance of the scene.	Few students in the group have an active role in the creation and performance of the scene.

MUSIC

Integrated Lesson Plan		Round and Round Strategy	
Content Area: Science	Fine Arts Area: Music	Lesson Title:	Form and Observation
Grade Level: K-2	Duration: 45-60 minutes	Teacher:	

Standards and Alignment

Content Area Standard(s):	Fine Arts Standard(s):
NGSS 1-LS3-1 Make observations to construct an evidence-based account that young plants and animals are like, but not exactly like, their parents.	Music: **Artistic Process:** Creating **Anchor Standard**: Generate and conceptualize artistic ideas and work.

Big Idea:	There are similarities and differences between parents and their offspring.	Essential Question	How are offspring alike and different from their parents?
21st Century Skills:	Creativity, Collaboration, Evaluate Information, Critical Thinking	Key Vocabulary:	Parents, offspring, similarities, differences, theme, variation

Vertical Alignment	Before Lesson:	During Lesson:	After Lesson:
	Identifying patterns in the natural and human world that can be observed.	Observing and describing through evidence how offspring are similar and different from their parents.	Analyzing and evaluating if an offspring is a match for a selected parent.

Materials List:	Recording of Twelve Variations of Vou dirai-je, Maman K.265/300e by Mozart, open space for movement, rhythm instruments (optional), animal scramble pictures (http://mlbean.byu.edu/Portals/26/docs/Animal%20Scramble%20babies%20and%20adult.pdf)

Instructional Delivery (guided, collaborative, and self-directed)

Student Learning Outcome(s):	I can observe same and different patterns.

Pre-Engagement:

Pre-assessment:

Review the Round and Round strategy with students using the song Twinkle Twinkle Little Star. Then, ask students to listen to Twelve Variations on Vous dirai-ja Maman (Twinkle, Twinkle Little Star) and raise their hand when they hear the part that repeats and always sounds the same. Identify this as the theme. Ask students if the parts that are not the theme sound the exact same, similar, or completely different than the theme (similar). This is called theme and variations. Ask students as a group to create a movement for the theme. Then, tell students that each time they hear the theme, they will dance that movement, and when they hear the variation, they can create their own motion.

Engagement:

Play the song again and then ask students to think about their individual motions on the variation. Were they similar to the Theme motion? Should they be? Repeat as needed.

Focal Lesson:	Give each child a picture from the Animal Scrambles Picture Sheet (http://mlbean.byu.edu/Portals/26/docs/Animal%20Scramble%20babies%20and%20adult.pdf) that you have cut. Each student must find their partner - each pair should have a baby animal and its matching adult animal. Ask students to identify as a pair what characteristics about their animals are the same and which are different. Discuss the class observations.
	Choose one animal (ie: the penguin) from the pictures and showcase the baby and adult version. Look at the items that were labeled "the same" and create a rhythm to clap for those items (ie: each time you say beak, flippers, or color = pat, clap, pat, clap). This is your theme. Any part that was different is your variation.
	Create a round using their themes for each animal. Have each group share their themes of similar traits between the adult and the baby and combine these themes to create a rhythmic song. Perform the rhythmic song all together, and then perform it as a round among the groups. When performed in the round, ask students: what sounded the same as when we did it together as a large group? What sounded different?

Integrated Assessment and Extension

Theme and Variation Composition

Explain that you will call out a body part of the selected animal. If it was something that was the same between the baby and adult, they will clap their "theme" rhythm. If it was something that was different, they can create their own 4-second rhythm. This is the variation. Remind them that the variation should sound similar to the theme, but not the same. Use a rubric for this closing exercise. The key assessment items should be Identifying same and different parts of an adult/child animal and performing theme and variation rhythms (are the variations similar to the main pattern?). Children should be scored on both items.

Suggested Grade-Band Extensions

3-5: Use the same activity, with a focus on siblings as multiple variations of inherited traits. Use musical compositions that are performed in a series, such as Karl Jenkins' Diamond Music, and discuss how each movement has similarities and difference among the movements, as well as to the main theme of the composition.

6-8: Use this same lesson structure to focus on mutations of a theme or set of genetic material. Utilize the Round and Round strategy to demonstrate this by having each group mutate the original theme in some way whenever they come into the round.

9-12: Use the lesson as an exploration into DNA as a set of coding instructions for character traits passed from parent to offspring. Analyze a musical counterpoint composition by Bach to identify the code for bringing in each newly stated theme.

Reflection Opportunities			
Student Reflections Prompts:	**Key Questions to Ask Students:** 1.How do we know if something is related? 2. What is the difference between a theme and its variations?	Teacher Reflection Prompts:	**Key Questions to Ask Yourself:** 1. Was there a seamless connection between the music and science in this lesson? 2. What pieces of this lesson were a challenge? Which pieces were most engaging for me and my students?

Form and Observation Pattern Assessment Rubric

Content Standard Assessed: **NGSS 1-LS3-1** Make observations to construct an evidence-based account that young plants and animals are like, but not exactly like, their parents.

Arts Standards Assessed: Music: **Artistic Process:** Creating **Anchor Standard**: Generate and conceptualize artistic ideas and work.

Assessment Item	3 (with excellence)	2 (with adequacy)	1 (with assistance)
Child can identify parts in an animal that are the same.			
Child can identify parts in an animal that are different			
Child can perform a theme in a piece of music			
Child can perform a variation on a theme that is similar to the theme but is not the same			

Total Score: _____/ 12

DANCE

Integrated Lesson Plan	Minute to Limit Strategy
Content Area: Math	Fine Arts Area: Dance	Lesson Title: **Bubble Solution**

Grade Level: K-2	Duration: 45 minutes	Teacher:

Standards and Alignment

Content Area Standard(s):	Fine Arts Standard(s):
CCSS.MATH.CONTENT.2.G.A.1 Recognize and draw shapes having specified attributes, such as a given number of angles or a given number of equal faces. Identify triangles, quadrilaterals, pentagons, hexagons, and cubes.	Dance: **Artistic Process:** Creating **Anchor Standard**: Organize and develop artistic ideas and work.

Big Idea:	Recognize and create shapes using the body	Essential Question:	How can we create shapes in various forms?
21st Century Skills:	Creativity, Collaboration, Evaluate Information, Critical Thinking	Key Vocabulary:	Shapes, space, energy, level

Vertical Alignment	Before Lesson:	During Lesson:	After Lesson:
	Identifying various shapes and their attributes.	Recognize and create shapes using movement and design.	Partition shapes using two, three or four equal shares.

Materials List:	Math Journals, pencils, homemade bubble solution (http://babyparenting.about.com/cs/activities/a/bubbles.htm), container, various items for creating bubble wands including: slotted spoon, funnels, fly swatters, mason jar lid rings, cookie cutters, wire hangers, pipe cleaners, straws and string

Instructional Delivery (guided, collaborative, and self-directed)

Student Learning Outcome(s):	I can find and create shapes using many different tools.

Pre-Engagement:	**Pre-assessment:**
	Review a variety of shapes and ask students to identify them upon sight. Include square, circle, rectangle, crescent, triangle, and octagon. Add others as appropriate.
	Engagement:
	Ask students to show each shape that was used for identification in the pre- assessment as the teacher calls them out with their bodies, both individually and in teams. Play a variety of music during this step that is both fast and slow. Use the Minute-to-Limit strategy when having students create the shapes in teams.

Focal Lesson:	Ask students to think about bubbles. What kind of shapes do they make? How fast or slow do they move? Are they loud or soft? Then, ask students to use their bodies to show what a bubble might look like and how it might move around the room. Ask students what would change the shape of a bubble. Show them a variety of bubble wands and ask them what about the wand might affect the shape of the bubble. Create a bubble solution with the students using the recipe found in the materials section of this seed. Then, ask students to dip your wands in, blow the bubbles and record the shapes they see in a math journal. Have students move like the bubbles they created with the bubble wands. Ask them to show the shapes with their bodies that they saw when they blew the bubbles. Remind them to use high, medium and low space just like the bubbles did as they floated.
Integrated Assessment and Extension	**Bubble Wand Designers** Have students create their own bubble wands using one of the options of materials you have provided. Their wand should showcase a shape of their choosing. Each student will work with a partner who will dance as the bubble from the wand while the other student blows the bubble.

| Integrated Assessment and Extension | **Suggested Grade-Band Extensions**

3-5: Use the same activity, with a focus on lines of symmetry. Students should dance in pairs with a line of symmetry between them. When creating their bubble wands, the bubbles should be pulled from the wands and joined together.

6-8: Using the standard for knowing formulas for the area and circumference of a circle, have students create a bubble using both their bodies and later, the bubble solution, which are measured by that formula.

9-12: Model with Geometry by creating a bubble solution that maximizes the size and speed of the bubbles produced. Identify and document the density, shape and speed of bubbles in the math journal. |

Reflection Opportunities

| Student Reflections Prompts: | **Key Questions to Ask Students:**
1. What attributes define each shape explored today?
2. What are some ways that you can create a shape? | Teacher Reflection Prompts: | **Key Questions to Ask Yourself:**
1. Was there a seamless connection between the dance and math in this lesson?
2. What pieces of this lesson were a challenge? Which pieces were most engaging for me and my students? |

Bubble Shapes Formative Assessment Rubric

Content Standard Assessed: **CCSS.MATH.CONTENT.2.G.A.1** Recognize and draw shapes having specified attributes, such as a given number of angles or a given number of equal faces. Identify triangles, quadrilaterals, pentagons, hexagons, and cubes.

Arts Standards Assessed: Dance: **Artistic Process:** Creating **Anchor Standard**: Organize and develop artistic ideas and work.

FOCAL ASSESSMENT QUESTIONS

Math: Can this student recognize and create shapes?
Dance: Can this student use shape and energy to demonstrate movement?

Math Look-Fors	Dance Look-Fors
☐ Student can recognize a variety of shapes as required by the grade-level	☐ Student can recognize shapes made through movement
◦ Student can create a variety of shapes as required by the grade-level	◦ Student can create a variety of shapes using their bodies
◦ Student can design shapes based upon their distinct attributes	◦ Student can apply artistic skill to create a shape that moves alone and with others
◦ Student can use space appropriately in their shape creation	◦ Student can use high, medium and low levels when moving their shapes

grades | 3-5

VISUAL ARTS

Integrated Lesson Plan	iNotice[3] Strategy	
Content Area: Science	Fine Arts Area: Visual Arts	Lesson Title: **Finger "Prints"**

Grade Level:	3-5	Duration:	45-60 minutes	Teacher:

Standards and Alignment

Content Area Standard(s):	Fine Arts Standard(s):
5-PS1-3. Make observations and measurements to identify materials based on their properties.	Visual Art: **Artistic Process:** Responding **Anchor Standard**: Perceive and analyze artistic work.

Big Idea:	Students use close observation to study and document the effect of different printing mediums.	Essential Question:	How can we express our learning through observation?
21st Century Skills:	Creativity, Collaboration, Problem Solving, Critical Thinking	Key Vocabulary:	observation, print, comparison

Vertical Alignment	Before Lesson:	During Lesson:	After Lesson:
	Engaging in close observation is an important part of the scientific method.	Observations provide data that may influence a solution or creative process.	Use observations from multiple sources to develop a theory of action.

Materials List:	Computer, Speakers, Internet Pencils, ink pads, paper, journals, Chuck Close Looking Guide (http://fristcenter.org/content/uploads/gallery_guides/chuck_close_looking_guide.pdf), photographs, Video (https://www.youtube.com/watch?v=fecOLyFyHV0), magnifying glass or microscope

Instructional Delivery (guided, collaborative, and self-directed)

Student Learning Outcome(s):	I can use observations to inform my understanding of the printing process.

Pre-Engagement:

Pre-assessment:

Students view Chuck Close's Fanny/Fingerpainting piece. Ask students to use the iNotice3 Strategy to read the artwork. Document the observations from students and chart as needed.

Engagement:

Ask students how they think the artwork was produced (a photograph, a drawing, etc?). After some discussion, reveal that the artist used his fingerprints to create the work. View some samples of Judith Braun's work and compare and contrast the works of both artists. View a video of Judith's process here: https://www.youtube.com/watch?v=fecOLyFyHV0

Focal Lesson:

Process:

Discuss why fingerprints are important (no two fingerprints are alike) and how else fingerprints might be used in the world today beyond artwork (ie:identification).

Provide students with ink pads and a clean piece of white paper. Demonstrate how to roll their finger print and ask them to roll their fingerprints onto the white paper. Then, provide students with magnifying glasses, or use an ExoLab microscope to view the fingerprints. **Note: if using the ExoLab microscope, attach it to an iPad and project student fingerprint samples onto a large screen.*

Focal Lesson:

Ask students to document their observations about each fingerprint. What patterns emerge? How are each different? Compare their fingerprints with their friends - what do they see? Identify the three main types of fingerprint patterns: loops, whorls and arches.

Ask students to create use the ink pads again to create a fingerprint, but this time, move the fingerprint in some way (drag, smudge, feather, etc). Observe through magnification what this does to the fingerprint pattern.

Break students into 4-6 groups. Give each group a photograph of an inanimate object. Ask students to document their observations about the photograph and determine what kinds of fingerprints would work best for the various parts of the object. Then, using their analysis of their own fingerprints, have students determine who's fingerprints will be used to recreate those selected parts of the image. For instance, if the stem of the flower should use a more whorled pattern of fingerprint, the students would choose a member of their group with a whorled fingerprint pattern. Students will also use their observations of what happens when fingerprints are manipulated (dragged, smudged, etc) to best recreate the photographed image. Both the fingerprint pattern and the fingerprint manipulation choices should be documented as part of the final product.

Integrated Assessment and Extension

Artist's Observation Statement: My Legacy

Students should each write an artist's statement about their completed fingerprint image that documents their observations of both the photograph and the fingerprints to determine the properties, style and elements used in their finished work. The statement should address how this work leaves their legacy for the world through their fingerprints.

Suggested Grade-Band Extensions

K-2: Create a fingerprint drawing using one fingerprint to explore the parts of a flower. Use different techniques (rolled, smudged, dragged) for different parts of the flower and identify each part through careful observation of living flowers or plants.

6-8: Explore the use of fingerprints through forensic investigations and create a piece of artwork that documents a forensic vignette.

9-12: Using actual forensic fingerprint evidence, use a photo editing software to cut out fingerprints to document the key suspects and how each suspect related to the case in a comprehensive piece of artwork.

Reflection Opportunities			
Student Reflection Prompts:	**Key Questions to Ask Students:** 1.Why is close observation important? 2. How can we use observation as a tool for creating something new?	Teacher Reflection Prompts:	**Key Questions to Ask Yourself:** 1. Was there a seamless connection between the art and science in this lesson? 2. What pieces of this lesson were a challenge? Which pieces were most engaging for me and my students?

Finger "Prints" Assessment Rubric

Content Standard Assessed: NGSS **5-PS1-3.** Make observations and measurements to identify materials based on their properties.

Arts Standards Assessed: Visual Art: **Artistic Process:** Responding **Anchor Standard**: Perceive and analyze artistic work.

Criteria	Distinguished Level (4)	Excelled Level (3)	Adequate Level (2)	Basic Level (1)
The Artist Statement clearly references evidence obtained throughout observations during the lesson	The student demonstrates in their statement use of sophisticated investigation and critical analysis.	The student demonstrates in their statement use of adequate investigation and critical analysis.	The student demonstrates in their statement some use of investigation and critical analysis.	The student demonstrates in their statement few, if any, references of investigation and critical analysis.
The Artist Statement identifies key art and science elements that contribute to the clarity of the finished project.	The student's use of key art and science elements are specific and accurate.	The student's use of key art and science elements are general and mostly accurate.	The student's use of key art and science elements are very broad and somewhat accurate.	The student's use of key art and science elements are vague and/or not accurate.

The student uses the Artist Statement to demonstrate that they can manipulate skills obtained during the lesson intentionally.	The student's statement provides direct evidence of scientific and artistic skills gained during the lesson and references these skills when discussing their work.	The student's statement provides general evidence of scientific and artistic skills gained during the lesson and references these skills when discussing their work.	The student's statement provides little evidence of scientific and artistic skills gained during the lesson and references these skills when discussing their work.	The student's statement provides no evidence of scientific and artistic skills gained during the lesson and does not reference these skills when discussing their work.
The Artist Statement demonstrates the student's ability to transfer knowledge into practice.	The student's statement reflects an ability to authentically connect two contents in a seamless way which demonstrates an extensive range of knowledge and skills.	The student's statement reflects an ability to authentically connect two contents in a clear way which demonstrates adequate knowledge of the topic.	The student's statement reflects connections that appear forced or may be unclear, but which demonstrate acceptable knowledge of the topic.	The student's statement represents a struggle to authentically connect two contents in a clear way which demonstrates adequate knowledge of the topic.

DRAMA

Integrated Lesson Plan | Human Flipbook Strategy

Content Area: Math	Fine Arts Area: Theatre	Lesson Title:	Interpreting Remainders

Grade Level: 3-5	Duration: 60-90 minutes	Teacher:

Standards and Alignment

Content Area Standard(s):	Fine Arts Standard(s):
CCSS.MATH.CONTENT.4.OA.A.3 Solve multistep word problems posed with whole numbers and having whole-number answers using the four operations, including problems in which remainders must be interpreted.	Theatre: **Artistic Process:** Performing **Anchor Standard**: Develop and refine artistic techniques and work for presentation.

Big Idea:	Interpreting remainders	Essential Question:	How do we solve a problem that includes a remainder?
21st Century Skills:	Creativity, Collaboration, Problem Solving, Critical Thinking	Key Vocabulary:	Remainder, actors' tools, tableau, division, multiplication, interpret

Vertical Alignment	Before Lesson:	During Lesson:	After Lesson:
	Understand what remainders are, and how they can be documented.	Interpret remainders through division and express this interpretation through performance	Represent the word problems using equations with a letter standing for the unknown quantity.

Materials List:	Actors' Tools (http://educationcloset.com/2013/05/31/actors-toolbox-script/) , paper, pencils, math resource books with a variety of word problems, camera, space for movement

Instructional Delivery (guided, collaborative, and self-directed)

Student Learning Outcome(s):	I can understand and interpret remainders with reasonableness.
Pre-Engagement:	**Pre-assessment:** Introduce the Actor's toolbox to students and go through each tools that students are familiar with their use. **Engagement:** Present a math problem for students that they need to solve without using their voice tools. IE: get yourselves into groups 3 within 10 seconds. If there is a remaining student(s), ask students what we could do with that remainder. Write their answers on the board.

Focal Lesson: Present a math lesson on interpreting remainders when dividing, using your math resource book as a guide. Look at how to do that process and then ask what is reasonable to do with the remainders? Have students solve 2 word problems as a group and 2 word problems independently. Think-pair-share their answers.

Have students get into groups of 3 or 5 and then pair each group with another team (2 groups of 3-5 people). Using one of the word problems they just completed, move students through the Human Flipbook Strategy in exploring the problem and defining a solution. One groups of students in the team should first create tableau using their body, concentration, imagination and cooperation tools that outline the 2 or 4 major points of the problem. Then, "flip" through the problem. The other group then creates the solution using the appropriate Actor's Tools and the Human Flipbook strategy - pairing their solution steps with the original steps outlines through the other group's flip book. One person is assigned to each step, which means that each group should have a "remainder" student. They must depict through their flipbook how to solve a problem with a remainder and how that remainder could be interpreted.

Repeat this process with a new word problem that has not yet been solved by the class. Each team must work through the problem using the flipbook and provide a solution, also through the flipbook strategy.

Take a photograph of each group and create a digital problem/solution flipbook sequence. Print or email a copy of the flipbook for students.

| Integrated Assessment and Extension | **Student Reflection Checklist**

Students should complete a reflection checklist and write their responses in the spaces provided for each group's drama presentation, citing evidence from the flipbook photograph sequence.

Suggested Grade-Band Extensions

K-2: Instead of interpreting remainders, try using this same lesson to teach how to use addition and subtraction within 20 to solve word problems that require adding to, taking from, putting together or taking apart.

6-8: Try using this lesson to apply the properties of operations to generate equivalent expressions.

9-12: Using real-world problems, use this lesson to help students develop a solution to systems of equations and/or inequalities and use the strategy as a way to interpret solutions as viable or non-viable options. |

Reflection Opportunities

| Student Reflection Prompts: | **Key Questions to Ask Students:**
1. What makes the interpretation of a remainder "reasonable"?
2. What are some ways that we can interpret a problem? | Teacher Reflection Prompts: | **Key Questions to Ask Yourself:**
1. Was there a seamless connection between the theatre and math in this lesson?
2. What pieces of this lesson were a challenge? Which pieces were most engaging for me and my students? |

Interpreting Remainders Assessment Rubric

Content Standard Assessed: **CCSS.MATH.CONTENT.4.OA.A.3** Solve multistep word problems posed with whole numbers and having whole-number answers using the four operations, including problems in which remainders must be interpreted.

Arts Standards Assessed: Theatre: **Artistic Process:** Performing **Anchor Standard**: Develop and refine artistic techniques and work for presentation.

Criteria	Student Response
Did the group use the Tableau and the Actors Tools to convey the problem-solving process? Provide evidence in your response. (4 points)	Points awarded: Evidence-based response:
Did the group use the remainder student in ways that were reasonable and which interpreted that remainder correctly? How so? (4 points)	Points awarded: Evidence-based response:

Did the problem flipbook and the solution flipbook tableaus correlate to each other? What went well here? What could be improved? (4 points)	Points awarded: Evidence-based response:
Based upon your experience in class, please explain what a remainder is and how it can be interpreted reasonably. Provide examples to justify your answer. (4 points)	Points awarded: Evidence-based response:

MUSIC

Integrated Lesson Plan | Improvisation Frame Strategy

Content Area: Math	Fine Arts Area: Music	Lesson Title: Musical Fractions

Grade Level: 3-5	Duration: 60 minutes	Teacher:

Standards and Alignment

Content Area Standard(s):	Fine Arts Standard(s):
CCSS.MATH.CONTENT.4.NF.B.3.A Understand addition and subtraction of fractions as joining and separating parts referring to the same whole.	Music: **Artistic Process:** Creating **Anchor Standard**: Organize and develop artistic ideas and work.

Big Idea:	Adding and Subtracting Fractions	Essential Question:	How can parts be manipulated to create a whole?
21st Century Skills:	Creativity, Collaboration, Problem Solving, Critical Thinking	Key Vocabulary:	Fraction, notation, quarter note, half note, whole note, equation, equivalent

Vertical Alignment	Before Lesson:	During Lesson:	After Lesson:
	Comparing fractions in reference to the same whole.	Adding fractions using standard music notation to equal a whole note's value.	Adding mixed numbers through equivalent fractions.

Materials List:	Musical chimes, boomwhackers, chart paper and markers or projection and recording technology for group discussion answers, cut and paste musical notes sheet (class created), clay or model magic

Instructional Delivery (guided, collaborative, and self-directed)

Student Learning Outcome(s):	I can read, write, and perform fraction sentences.

Pre-Engagement:	**Pre-assessment:** Discuss and review music notes as sounding fast or slow and why. i.e: some notes are held longer or some notes are held for a shorter duration. Discuss and review the duration for 1/2, 1/4, and whole notes. Discuss and review sizes of each note as a fraction when comparing to each other.

Focal Lesson:

Engagement:

Have a clay cutting activity in whole group on the carpet. Ask students what happens when we put the 2, 3, or 4 pieces back together. Discuss equivalence that 2 halves equal 1 whole just as 3 thirds equal 1 whole etc. Show the boomwhackers and discuss the visual comparisons of fractions. Ask students which may make a higher sound or a lower sound based on size. What makes you say that? How would you compare the boomwhackers as fractions?

Process:

In a large group, discuss equivalencies from the clay demonstration. The teacher will write the answers on the chart paper. Example: "2 pieces that are equal in size are equivalent to 1 whole and 4 pieces equal in size are equivalent to one whole".

The teacher will then demonstrate how to use the instruments. Ask students to experiment with the instruments and then to play their instrument and count to 4 in their heads before making the sound become silent. A note that you hold for 4 beats in this sentence is a whole note. How would you write that as a number? (1, because it is 1 whole number). Then ask: what if we split that whole note into two equal parts? What kind of notes would be have (half notes)? How would you write those notes as a number (1/2)? How would you play those two notes? Have students experiment with play half notes and whole notes on their instruments. Then ask, what if we split those two half notes into two equal parts? What kind of notes would you have (quarter notes)? And how would you write that as a number (1/4)?

Then students in small groups will try each note to get a feel for how the notes and chimes work using the information they have about fractions.

Perform – one group of three students at a time, will show one whole by tapping the chime and saying "whole-note-four-beats," where each word is one beat. Repeated by each group for ¼ ("quarter, quarter, quarter, quarter") and ½ ("half-note; half-note").

Perform – using the improvisation frame, students create a note sentence that is equal to one whole note. Students can create their note sentence using any combination of quarter, half or whole note values. Each student will perform their sentence while the rest of the class is providing the frame of quarter, half and whole notes.

Integrated Assessment and Extension

Musical Fractions Worksheet

Students should complete the musical fractions worksheet and will be assessed on the following items: identifying fractions as equivalent to musical notes, matching notes to the correct fractions, adding fractions correctly to equal a whole number.

Suggested Grade-Band Extensions

K-2: Use the same lesson, but instead of adding fractions, add the number of beats. So two half notes would each 2 (beats) + 2 (beats) = 4 beats.

Reflection Opportunities

Student Reflection Prompts:	Key Questions to Ask Students:	Teacher Reflection Prompts:	Key Questions to Ask Yourself:
	1.What are some ways you can add fractions? 2. How can you add fractions with different denominators?		1. Was there a seamless connection between the music and math in this lesson? 2. What pieces of this lesson were a challenge? Which pieces were most engaging for me and my students?

Musical Fractions Worksheet

Name _____ Date _____

1.Draw a whole note.

2. Draw a quarter note.

3. Draw a half note.

4. How much is one quarter note and one quarter note? ¼ + ¼ = _____

5. How much is one half note and one half note?

½ + ½ = _____

6. How much is one whole note and one whole note? 1 + 1 = _____

Write the following patterns as a fraction sentence:

7. Quarter note, quarter note, half note:

8. Half note, half note:

Fill in the blanks to make an equivalent fraction sentence:

9. 1/4 + _____ = 1

10. 1/2 + _____ + _____ = _____

Write your own note pattern that equals one whole note and show the fraction of the notes you used in your pattern.

The most important thing I learned from doing musical fractions is….

I liked/disliked learning about fractions with musical instruments because…..

DANCE

Integrated Lesson Plan| Movement Vocabulary Strategy

Content Area: Science	Fine Arts Area: Movement	Lesson Title:	Moving Constellations
Grade Level: 3-5	Duration:	60-90 minutes	Teacher:

Standards and Alignment

Content Area Standard(s):	Fine Arts Standard(s):
5-ESS1-2. Represent data in graphical displays to reveal patterns of daily changes in length and direction of shadows, day and night, and the seasonal appearance of some stars in the night sky.	Dance: **Artistic Process:** Performing **Anchor Standard**: Analyze, interpret and select artistic work for presentation.

Big Idea:	Patterns can be identified in the night sky.	Essential Question:	How are constellations represented?
21st Century Skills:	Creativity, Collaboration, Problem Solving, Critical Thinking	Key Vocabulary:	Stars, constellation, astronomer, adjective

Vertical Alignment	Before Lesson:	During Lesson:	After Lesson:
	Constellations were charted as a way of mapping the night sky	Constellations are stars which form a shape in the night sky which can change depending upon the season	Use analysis to demonstrate daily changes between night and day through shadows and the seasonal appearance of some stars

Materials List:	Dance elements poster (http://educationcloset.com/wp-content/uploads/2011/07/elements-of-dance.pdf), chart paper and markers or digital writing tools and projection, Glow in the Dark Constellations book, MP3/CD Player, Aurora Borealis Concerto Movement 3, open space for movement

Instructional Delivery (guided, collaborative, and self-directed)

Student Learning Outcome(s):	I can demonstrate how the night sky changes depending upon the season
Pre-Engagement:	**Pre-assessment:** Students view images of constellations in the sky at night, trace the connections between the stars and describe what shapes, characters or stories come to mind. **Engagement:** Read the book "Glow in the Dark Constellations". Read the introduction as a whole group and then split the class into 5-6 small groups. Assign each group a constellation found within the book. After reading, have all groups share out to the whole class.

| Focal Lesson: | View the constellations from the book again, in a selected season (i.e.: The Big Dipper in the summer sky) and ask students to describe what shapes or patterns they see in this depiction of the constellation. Then, view the same constellation in a different season's sky. Identify similarities and differences to the constellation image from earlier. |

Ask students to think about the phrases or words they would associate with the images of each constellation for each season. i.e: the cup looks like it's pouring in summer; the cup is dipping in the winter.

Using the Movement Vocabulary strategy, create a table chart with the columns "season", "constellation", "description", and "dance element" and fill in with each of the answers. For instance, an example might be "Winter", "The Big Dipper", "Dipping", "Curved Shape"

Then, tell students that you will be playing a piece of music and they will move around the room. When the music stops, you will call out a constellation and its season and they will need to show what the descriptor looks like with their bodies in a frozen position using the dance element. For example, when stating "Big Dipper in Winter" students would need to use their bodies in a curved shape to show "dipping" *Musical suggestion: Aurora Borealis Concerto Movement 3.*

Closing:
Do the movement to the music again, but this time when the music stops, students will need to form the selected constellation in groups of 4-5 that portrays what the descriptor might look like using the dance element selected.

Integrated Assessment and Extension	**Movement Constellation Map** Students can work collaboratively to show the movement of the constellations in the night sky dependent upon the seasons. In groups of 4-5, students will be given a constellation that changes position in the night sky based upon the season. Mark off a circle in the room and identify North, South, East and West. Have students plot their constellation on the circle for all four seasons. Then, students will create their constellation with their bodies starting with spring and move as the teacher announces the change of season. They will need to ensure that they move together, keeping an appropriate space between themselves and other students. **Suggested Grade-Band Extensions** **K-2:** Instead of using constellations, use this same lesson with a focus on the moon and its changing phases. **6-8:** Try using this lesson to explore the effect of gravity on the solar system. **9-12:** Use this lesson as a way for students to construct a model of explanation of the Big Bang Theory.

Reflection Opportunities			
Student Reflection Prompts:	**Key Questions to Ask Students:** 1. Do constellations move? 2. Why do we chart the location of the stars?	Teacher Reflection Prompts:	**Key Questions to Ask Yourself:** 1. Was there a seamless connection between the dance and science in this lesson? 2. What pieces of this lesson were a challenge? Which pieces were most engaging for me and my students?

Moving Constellations Checklist Assessment

Content Standard Assessed: **5-ESS1-2.** Represent data in graphical displays to reveal patterns of daily changes in length and direction of shadows, day and night, and the seasonal appearance of some stars in the night sky.

Arts Standards Assessed: Dance: **Artistic Process:** Performing **Anchor Standard**: Analyze, interpret and select artistic work for presentation

FOCAL ASSESSMENT QUESTIONS

Science: Can this student represent the change of the constellations in the night sky based upon the seasons?

Dance: Can this student create a sequence of movements in relationship to others on a central theme?

Science Look-Fors	Dance Look-Fors
☐ Student can recognize a series of constellations	☐ Student can recognize and use different dance elements to create a shape
☐ Student can identify the constellation in a variety of different positions	○ Student can identify their spot for movement in a sequence of choreographed steps
○ Student can identify where constellations are located in different seasons	○ Student can alter their shape dependent upon its location in the performance space
○ Student can create an accurate map of the night sky in various seasons	○ Student can create a movement sequence that accurately depicts constellations in the night sky over four seasons

grades | 6-8

VISUAL ARTS

Integrated Lesson Plan	6 Dots of Separation Strategy	
Content Area: Math	Fine Arts Area: Visual Arts	Lesson Title: Proportionate People
Grade Level: 6-8	Duration: (2) 45-60 minute class periods	Teacher:

Standards and Alignment

Content Area Standard(s):	Fine Arts Standard(s):
CCSS.MATH.CONTENT.7.RP.A.2 Recognize and represent proportional relationships between quantities.	Visual Art: **Artistic Process:** Responding **Anchor Standard**: Perceive and analyze artistic work.

Big Idea:	Proportion can effect perception.	Essential Question:	How can you use proportion to manipulate perception?
21st Century Skills:	Creativity, Collaboration, Evaluate Information, Critical Thinking, Problem-Solving	Key Vocabulary:	Proportion, ratios, stippling, landmarks, grid, emphasis, perception

Vertical Alignment	Before Lesson:	During Lesson:	After Lesson:
	Computation of unit rates associated with ratios.	Identifying, calculating and creating proportional relationships.	Use proportional relationships to solve a multi-step percentage problem.

Materials List:	Pencils, grid paper, colored pencils, markers, tape, photos of historic landmarks from around the world, images of men, women and children.

Instructional Delivery (guided, collaborative, and self-directed)

Student Learning Outcome(s):	I can create a proportional relationship between a person and a landmark that effects perception by the viewer.
Pre-Engagement:	**Pre-assessment:** View a variety of images of famous landmarks from around the world (The Eiffel Tower, The Statue of Liberty, The Taj Mahal, etc). Ask students how large or small they think the landmark is based only on it's place within the image. Then, show images with people in front of or beside the landmark. Are these people proportionate in the image to the landmark itself? Why or why not? **Engagement:** Provide the height measurements of each landmark and the height measurements for an average male, female and child. Ask students to represent the proportional relationship of the landmark to a man, woman and child by an equation.

Focal Lesson: Provide each student with an image of one of the landmarks and a piece of grid paper. Ask students to represent the proportional relationship they calculated in the engagement by measuring the landmarks based on the amount of blocks on the grid it consumes (i.e.: the Eiffel Tower is 20 grid blocks in height) and then shading in these blocks.

Using a different color, shade in the amount of blocks that an average male, female and child would consume on the grid based upon their earlier equation. (i.e: a male would represent 1 block on the grid).

Discuss how you can change the proportional relationship between objects based upon how the image was captured (i.e.: a close up of a person in front of the Pyramids at Giza could make the pyramids look smaller and the person look larger). How does this change in proportional relationship effect reality?

Overlay the original landmark image with a piece of grid paper and use the Stippling technique to transfer the landmark onto the grid paper. Do this same process with a picture of a male, female or child.

Have students create a stippled composite image that combines the landmark and either the man, woman or child in a skewed proportional relationship compared to the original. Once completed, ask students to calculate the new proportional relationship between the individual and the landmark.

Integrated Assessment and Extension	**Proportionate Mural**

Upon completion, have students create a mural using their proportionate people and landmark grids. As they select where to place each of their landmarks, students can measure their entire image in proportion to their neighboring image. For instance, if the man in front of the Statue of Liberty is next to the woman beside the Eiffel Tower on the mural, what is the proportional relationship between the two images as a whole? Have the students work collaboratively to create the proportional relationship equations and write them in between the two images. Each student is responsible for developing and/or checking at least 4 equations. They can initial each equation they have created or checked for accuracy. Additionally, for each image created, students must write a sentence that describes how the proportional relationship is meant to effect the perception of the image by the audience.

Suggested Grade-Band Extensions

K-2: Use this same activity, without the added element of people. Focusing solely on the landmarks, ask students to order the landmarks by length and then use the 6 Dots of Separation Strategy to recreate each landmark as either smaller, larger or the same size as the original. Reclassify the new landmarks created using the strategy.

3-5: Students can create a scaled version of the landmarks using the 6 Dots of Separation Strategy to reimagine their scaled images.

9-12: Using the same lesson design, utilize photo editing software rather than grid paper to create a digital version of the images.

Reflection Opportunities			
Student Reflections Prompts:	**Key Questions to Ask Students:** 1.How does a proportional relationship effect perception about an object? 2. How can we manipulate perception using proportional relationships?	Teacher Reflection Prompts:	**Key Questions to Ask Yourself:** 1. Was there a seamless connection between the art and math in this lesson? 2. What pieces of this lesson were a challenge? Which pieces were most engaging for me and my students?

Proportionate People Assessment Rubric

Content Standard Assessed: **CCSS.MATH.CONTENT.7.RP.A.2** Recognize and represent proportional relationships between quantities.

Arts Standards Assessed: Visual Art: **Artistic Process:** Responding **Anchor Standard**: Perceive and analyze artistic work.

Criteria	Distinguished Level (4)	Excelled Level (3)	Adequate Level (2)	Basic Level (1)
The proportionate relationship equations between landmarks are accurate	The proportional relationship equations between the landmarks are all correct.	The proportional relationship equations between the landmarks are mostly correct.	Some of the proportional relationship equations between the landmarks are correct.	None of the proportional relationship equations between the landmarks are correct.
The artist sentence for the created image reflects an understanding of the effect of proportion on the perception of the viewer.	The student's sentence reflects a thoughtful decision in choosing how to share their meaning through the finished work.	The student's sentence reflects a decision in choosing how to share their meaning through the finished work.	The student's sentence reflects an understanding of their meaning through the finished work, though it may be rushed or broad.	The student's sentence reflects a need for further growth and understanding of the topic in order to share their meaning through the finished work.

The student uses the artist sentence and subsequent equations through the mural to demonstrate that they can manipulate skills obtained during the lesson intentionally.	The student's sentence and equations provides direct evidence of math and artistic skills gained during the lesson and references these skills through the production of their mural.	The student's sentence and equations provides general evidence of math and artistic skills gained during the lesson and references these skills through the production of their mural.	The student's sentence and equations provides little evidence of math and artistic skills gained during the lesson and references these skills through the production of their mural.	The student's sentence and equations provides no evidence of scientific and artistic skills gained during the lesson and does not reference these skills through the production of their mural.
The mural demonstrates the student's ability to transfer knowledge into practice.	The student's mural contribution reflects an ability to authentically connect two contents in a seamless way which demonstrates an extensive range of knowledge and skills.	The student's mural contribution reflects an ability to authentically connect two contents in a clear way which demonstrates adequate knowledge of the topic.	The student's mural contribution reflects connections that appear forced or may be unclear, but which demonstrate acceptable knowledge of the topic.	The student's mural contribution represents a struggle to authentically connect two contents in a clear way which demonstrates adequate knowledge of the topic.

DRAMA

Integrated Lesson Plan | If/Then Strategy

Content Area: Science	Fine Arts Area: Theatre	Lesson Title: Reactive Fireworks

Grade Level: 6-8	Duration: 45-60 minutes	Teacher:

Standards and Alignment

Content Area Standard(s):	Fine Arts Standard(s):
MS-PS1-2. Analyze and interpret data on the properties of substances before and after the substances interact to determine if a chemical reaction has occurred.	Theatre: **Artistic Process:** Creating **Anchor Standard**: Generate and conceptualize artistic ideas and work.

Big Idea:	Understanding and predicting chemical reactions	Essential Question:	How is energy involved chemical processes?
21st Century Skills:	Creativity, Collaboration, Problem Solving, Critical Thinking	Key Vocabulary:	Energy, reaction, formula, oxidizer, compound

Vertical Alignment	Before Lesson:	During Lesson:	After Lesson:
	Defining and viewing examples of energy	Exploring the chemical reaction process through the transfer of energy	Experimenting with chemical reactions that store energy and that release energy

Materials List:	Smithsonian article: (http://www.smithsonianmag.com/science-nature/5-things-you-didnt-know-about-the-science-of-fireworks-481649/?no-ist=) , salt, white watercolor paper, watercolor paint, water and brushes, journal and pencil

Instructional Delivery (guided, collaborative, and self-directed)

Student Learning Outcome(s):	I can analyze and interpret an experiment to determine if a chemical reaction has occurred.
Pre-Engagement:	**Pre-assessment:** Discuss experiences students have had with fireworks displays. Include unique displays they have seen, where they viewed the displays, and what questions they have about displays. Sample questions might include: *What makes the colors? How do they create the designs? How do they time everything to the music?* **Engagement:** Read the Smithsonian article 5 Things You Didn't Know about the Science of Fireworks. Ask students to think-pair-share with a neighbor about the article and if it answered any of the questions brought up during the class discussion.

Focal Lesson: Discuss the chemical reaction that takes place when the charge is ignited to transfer energy from the main fuel to the colorant chemicals. Move through the If/Then strategy as a whole group. Ask students to split into two groups. One group is the fuel and the other is the colorant chemicals. As the teacher, you will act as the charge.

Ask students: if I ignite the fuel group, then what will happen? Brainstorm together based upon their knowledge from the Smithsonian article. Then, have students act out the reaction of transferring energy from the fuel to the chemicals. Discuss the level of energy that is being conveyed by their bodies during their movement - is this indicative of the energy that fuel would carry to the chemicals?

Tell the students to pause and ask: if the fuel's energy is transferred to the chemicals, then the chemicals....? Again, allow students to brainstorm and act out their response. Discuss the level of energy that their bodies produced as chemicals in response to the fuel. Is this also indicative of the chemical reaction of the colorant in response to the fuel?

Using the If/Then strategy again, ask students to think about their knowledge of chemical reactions thus far and what happens when energy is transferred. Tell students that they will be using watercolor paint to create a firework design. Ask students: If you are the paint and I were to place salt directly beside you then… and have students react with their bodies as a prediction to what the paint will do.

Pair up students and give each pair a plain piece of white watercolor paper, 3 colors of watercolor paint, a straw and some salt. Ask students to paint a fireworks design of shapes on their paper.

Have students add salt strategically to each firework line or shape immediately while the paint is still wet and to write their observations of the reaction with the paint on a separate piece of paper. Then, ask students to use the straw to gently blow the paint toward the salt. Again, have students write their observations. Create a series of if/then statements to describe the chemical reactions of their experiment.

Integrated Assessment and Extension

Dramatic Fireworks Display

Students will perform their if/then statements as a fireworks display drama. The teacher will act as narrator for each team and each student performs either the "if" or the "then" of their observation. Their performances should clearly demonstrate their understanding of the process of chemical reactions and how energy plays a role in this process. Students will assess their peers' performances using a rubric.

Suggested Grade-Band Extensions

K-2: Instead of fireworks, focus on color absorption instead and use the if/then strategy to predict and share observations about what happens when stems are added to a container of water with food coloring. Discuss how the root structure of the plant will carry the color into the plant.

3-5: Try using this lesson outline for studying electricity. Use the same process, but substitute experiments for this type of energy transfer.

9-12: Have students use the if/then strategy to help them design a new kind of firework display, that also takes into account the musical timing and variation of color.

Reflection Opportunities			
Student Reflection Prompts:	**Key Questions to Ask Students:** 1.What causes a chemical reaction? 2. What are some ways that energy is transferred?	Teacher Reflection Prompts:	**Key Questions to Ask Yourself:** 1. Was there a seamless connection between the theatre and science in this lesson? 2. What pieces of this lesson were a challenge? Which pieces were most engaging for me and my students?

Reactive Fireworks Checklist Assessment Rubric

Content Standard Assessed: **MS-PS1-2.** Analyze and interpret data on the properties of substances before and after the substances interact to determine if a chemical reaction has occurred.

Arts Standards Assessed: Theatre: **Artistic Process:** Creating **Anchor Standard**: Generate and conceptualize artistic ideas and work.

Criteria	Student Response
Did the performance demonstrate a clear example of the chemical response process? Provide evidence in your response. (4 points)	Points awarded: Evidence-based response:
Did the performance explicitly demonstrate a transfer of energy? How so? (4 points)	Points awarded: Evidence-based response:
Did the performers' use of energy and expression correlate in equal measure to the levels demonstrated in the actual experiment? Provide evidence in your response. (4 points)	Points awarded: Evidence-based response:
Based upon your experience in class, please explain how this group's experiment and performance demonstrates the chemical reaction process based upon energy transfer. Provide examples to justify your answer. (4 points)	Points awarded: Evidence-based response:

DANCE

Integrated Lesson Plan | Mirroring Strategy

Content Area: Math	Fine Arts Area: Dance	Lesson Title: Dancing Angles
Grade Level: 6-8	Duration: 60-90 minutes	Teacher:

Standards and Alignment

Content Area Standard(s):	Fine Arts Standard(s):
CCSS.MATH.CONTENT.8.G.A. Understand congruence and similarity using physical models, transparencies, or geometry software.	Dance: **Artistic Process:** Creating **Anchor Standard**: Organize and develop artistic ideas and work

Big Idea:	Identify the congruence of angles in relationship with one another	Essential Question:	How can you manipulate angles to be congruent?
21st Century Skills:	Creativity, Collaboration, Problem Solving, Critical Thinking, Innovation	Key Vocabulary:	Acute, right, obtuse, angle, wedge, polygon, degree, pattern, repetition, contrast, balance, variety and unity/harmony

Vertical Alignment	Before Lesson:	During Lesson:	After Lesson:
	Identification and measurement of acute, obtuse and right angles	Manipulating the congruence between two or more shapes using parallel lines, line segments and angles of the same measure	Describing the effects of translations, rotations and rotations using coordinates
Materials List:	LCD projector/SMART Board, See, Think, Wonder Chart, internet connection, computer, speakers, video recorders or cell phones (optional), iMovie or other video editing software (optional), Synchronous Objects (http://synchronousobjects.osu.edu/content.html#/fullVideoScore)		

Instructional Delivery (guided, collaborative, and self-directed)

Student Learning Outcome(s):	I can create a choreographed dance that demonstrates congruence between partners.

Pre-Engagement:

Pre-assessment:

Allow students to watch 2-3 minutes of The Dance from the website http://synchronousobjects.osu.edu/ content.html#/fullVideoScore Ask students to write down what they see, what they think and what they wonder about the video clip. Students may share out with the whole group from each column. Write these ideas down for the class.

Engagement:

Ask students to view the video again, but this time to raise their hands each time they see an angle. Upon raising their hands, pause the video and ask students to identify the angle, line or line segment that they see. Students should write down these answers, along with a visual representation of what is being identified (i.e.: if an acute angle is identified, students should draw an acute angle and label it as such)

Focal Lesson:

Ask students to get into pairs and to select one of the angles that they identified from the video. As pairs, students should use the Mirroring Strategy to create this angle in congruence with each other.

Partners will then get into a larger group with two other sets of partners who had the same angle. As a group of 6, they must now work together to create the same angle, while keeping congruent lines throughout their movement. What was challenging about this exercise?

Hang 2 large pieces of bulletin board paper (6' by 4' at least) somewhere in the room. Ask students to get back into their original pairs. The teacher will tell students that they will listen to a piece of ambient music, similar to what they saw in The Dance, and that one partner will move to the music using their body to create angles and arcs in front of one piece of paper. The other partner will trace the angles onto the paper. Students will form two lines of pairs. Each pair will have approximately 30 seconds to complete their dance angle traces. When their time is complete, they will go back to their seats. The music is found here: Play the ambient music "The Storm Within", found at this site: http://www.dreamstate.to/audio/the_storm_within.mp3

Students will then measure their own angle and draw a mirrored congruent angle directly on the paper.

Integrated Assessment and Extension	**Angled Choreography**

Angled Choreography

As a class, create a choreographed dance of congruent angles. Write the choreography and identify the angles being used. Perform the dance with the ambient music originally used in class. If possible, record the dance as a video and play back for students to identify their use of congruent angles throughout the piece. As an extension, students may upload the recording to a piece of software, such as iMovie, and add images of the identified angles to appear during the dance, similar to the Synchronous Objects video from the beginning. If this is done, the measurements of the angles should also be added to the video.

Suggested Grade-Band Extensions

K-2: Use the lesson to focus on analyzing, comparing, creating and composing shapes with their bodies. Instead of focusing on angles, focus on the larger shapes being made through the dance.

3-5: Try using this lesson to explore lines of symmetry when creating mirrored angles and defining the vertices within the angle.

9-12: Use this same lesson, but adjust it to include the use of a transversal crossing a parallel line. Have students measure the angles with the transversal to test for congruency in corresponding angles.

Reflection Opportunities

Student Reflections Prompts:	Key Questions to Ask Students:	Teacher Reflection Prompts:	Key Questions to Ask Yourself:
	1.What makes something congruent? 2. What is the difference between congruence and parallel?		1. Was there a seamless connection between the dance and math in this lesson? 2. What pieces of this lesson were a challenge? Which pieces were most engaging for me and my students?

Dancing Angles Checklist Assessment

Content Standard Assessed: **CCSS.MATH.CONTENT.8.G.A.** Understand congruence and similarity using physical models, transparencies, or geometry software.

Arts Standards Assessed: Dance: **Artistic Process:** Creating **Anchor Standard**: Organize and develop artistic ideas and work

FOCAL ASSESSMENT QUESTIONS

Math: Can this student demonstrate understanding of congruent angles?

Dance: Can this student create a choreography sequence which is based upon congruent angles?

Math Look-Fors	Dance Look-Fors
☐ Student can define congruence	☐ Student can recognize the appearance of angles in body movement
☐ Student can correctly identify congruent angles	◦ Student can correctly identify dance elements needed to create an angle
◦ Student can create a congruent angle accurately	◦ Student can create a congruent angle accurately with their body
◦ Student can measure a congruent angle with accuracy	◦ Student can develop a sequence of choreography that highlights congruent angles

grades | 9-12

VISUAL ARTS

Integrated Lesson Plan | Whose Line is it Anyway Strategy

Content Area: Technology	Fine Arts Area: Visual Arts	Lesson Title: Font Marketing
Grade Level: 9-12	Duration: 60-90 minutes	Teacher:

Standards and Alignment

Content Area Standard(s):	Fine Arts Standard(s):
NETS for Students 3: Students use productivity tools to collaborate in constructing technology-enhanced models, prepare publications, and produce creative works.	Visual Art: **Artistic Process:** Creating **Anchor Standard**: Generate and conceptualize artistic ideas and work.

Big Idea:	Fonts use design principles to convey a message	Essential Question:	How are fonts used to deliver a message or idea?
21st Century Skills:	Creativity, Collaboration, Evaluate Information, Analyze Media, Create Media Product	Key Vocabulary:	Font, typography, geometric, symmetry, serif, sans-serif, elements of design

Vertical Alignment	Before Lesson:	During Lesson:	After Lesson:
	Understanding how and why media messages are constructed	Using the knowledge about media messages to create a font that is representative of an artist and can brand that artist's work	Create a marketing campaign for the artist that uses the font created in a variety of media settings using technology to support its implementation
Materials List:	Pencils, list of famous artists and selected works to explore, computers, fontstruct.com, typography infographic: http://www.bestinfographics.co/serif-vs-sans-serif-fonts-infographic/serif-vs-sans-serif-font-infographic/, Kandinsky Font article: http://www.visualnews.com/2012/07/26/typography-kandinsky-style/, various headline samples, easel.ly		

Instructional Delivery (guided, collaborative, and self-directed)

Student Learning Outcome(s):	I can develop a new font inspired by an artist.

Pre-Engagement:

Pre-assessment:

Examine a series of headlines. Ask students what messages the headlines are trying to convey to the audience. Move beyond the headline itself and explore the subliminal messages being shared from the headline. Is it a call to action? Is it based in background knowledge? What does it make you feel or think? Share the same set of headings, this time being written in a different font. Do the headings have the same impact? Why or why not?

Engagement:

Explore the basics of font design using this info graphic: http://www.bestinfographics.co/serif-vs-sans-serif-fonts-infographic/serif-vs-sans-serif-font-infographic/ How are the elements of design being utilized for typography? Ask students to look again at the headlines and select a font that would better convey its message, based upon the information they just read. How does print and multimedia use technology to produce a marketing campaign?

Focal Lesson:

Share with students the article, Typography: Kandinsky Style, located here: http://www.visualnews.com/2012/07/26/typography-kandinsky-style/ and think-pair-share their thoughts on how the font represents the work of the famed artist. Discuss how technology could be used to market this artist using the created font (youtube video, Facebook page, print media, etc).

Ask students to think about their own favorite artist. If they claim to not have one, give them some time to research a variety of artists from a pre-populated list to find one that may appeal to them in some way. Once they have selected their artist, have them write down the name of the artist on a piece of paper. Ask: what feelings, actions, or thoughts do you wish to convey about this artist? Write all of these down.

Working collaboratively with a partner, move through the Whose Line is it Anyway strategy to help create a font that is representative of the chosen artist. Use of the knowledge gained about serif/san-serif fonts, purpose behind typography, and the information about the Kandinsky font should be captured throughout this activity.

Once happy with the outcome, students will then use the website http://fontstruct.com or a font-creation software program to bring their font and artist to life.

Integrated Assessment and Extension	**Font Infographic** When finished, have students create an infographic using either a photo editing software or easel.ly that highlights their process of creating their new artist-inspired font. Include if it is using serif or sans-serif, why those choices were made, how the font is representative of the artist, and how technology can be utilized to both support the font's creation and market the artist and their work. **Suggested Grade-Band Extensions** **K-2:** Show images from Kandinsky and then show the font with his name. Ask students to identify similarities and differences. Then, ask students to create a piece of art that uses shapes like Kandinsky. Ask them to choose one of the shapes from their artwork and use the Whose Line is it Anyway Strategy to recreate it and change it in some way. Then, use the fontstruct.com website to create an image that looks like the shape they created. **3-5:** Students can move through the modified K-2 lesson, but they can create their entire name as an artist in the fontstruct.com website. **6-8**: These students can move through the same lesson as the 9-12 band, without needing to create an infographic. Their assessment can be the translation of their font from written form to digital form.

Reflection Opportunities			
Student Reflections Prompts:	**Key Questions to Ask Students:** 1.How are fonts used to convey a message? 2. How does print and multimedia use technology to market these messages?	Teacher Reflection Prompts:	**Key Questions to Ask Yourself:** 1. Was there a seamless connection between the art and technology in this lesson? 2. What pieces of this lesson were a challenge? Which pieces were most engaging for me and my students?

Font Marketing Formative Assessment Rubric

Content Standard Assessed: **NETS for Students 3:** Students use productivity tools to collaborate in constructing technology-enhanced models, prepare publications, and produce creative works.

Arts Standards Assessed: Visual Art: **Artistic Process:** Creating **Anchor Standard**: Generate and conceptualize artistic ideas and work.

FOCAL ASSESSMENT QUESTIONS

Technology: Can this student use technology to create a font that is representative of an artist?

Art: Can this student create an artistic work that brings their original idea to life?

Technology Look-Fors	Art Look-Fors
☐ Student can identify serif and sans-serif typography and their uses	☐ Student can showcase their understanding of the elements of design in their finished work
○ Student can develop a font that uses the elements of typography to capture an artist's body of work	○ Student can demonstrate an understanding and synthesis of an artist's body of work
○ Student can develop an infographic which graphically explains their choices in the creation of their new font	○ Student can apply artistic skill to create an infographic that is both informative and easy to navigate
○ Student can use technology, such as fontstruct.com and easel.ly.com as a tool for design manipulation	○ Student can use artistic skill when making choices for designing a new font

MUSIC

Integrated Lesson Plan		Play and Tell Strategy	
Content Area: Science	Fine Arts Area: Music	Lesson Title:	Producing Beats
Grade Level: 9-12	Duration: 45 minutes	Teacher:	

Standards and Alignment

Content Area Standard(s):	Fine Arts Standard(s):
HS-ETS1-4. Use a computer simulation to model the impact of proposed solutions to a complex real-world problem with numerous criteria and constraints on interactions within and between systems relevant to the problem.	**MU:Cr1-T.II.a:** (Imagine) Explore sounds and compose or improvise multiple musical ideas, excerpts, melodies, or arrangements that exhibit originality, unity and variety for a specific purpose or to express intent, personal interests or experiences using digital tools and resources.

Big Idea:	Students explore the engineering process through music mixing and editing.	Essential Question:	How do we problem solve?
21st Century Skills:	Creativity, Collaboration, Evaluate Information, Analyze Media, Create Media Product	Key Vocabulary:	layering, engineer, musical elements, texture

Vertical Alignment	Before Lesson:	During Lesson:	After Lesson:
	Compositions have a natural sequence.	Music can be engineered to create composition development.	Use their knowledge of texture to deepen a composition's development.

Materials List:	Computer, Speakers, Internet, Pencils, Pens, Journals, Copies of Poems (http://www.poets.org/ page.php/prmID/86), Microphones (if not included internally), Video (http://www.youtube.com/watch?v=aNuD0U84NXk)

Instructional Delivery (guided, collaborative, and self-directed)

Student Learning Outcome(s):	I can use music to engineer story development.
Pre-Engagement:	**Pre-assessment:** Students listen to a variety of live and studio version music pieces and use "Play and Tell" to describe their observations of the music influence over the song's core intent. For instance, a studio version of "Hey Jude" vs. a live version of the same song, "Play and Tell" the essence of the difference to the song's intent. **Engagement:** Engage students in a discussion about their ideas on why music sounds different live vs. in the studio. Watch the 4-minute video about mixing and mastering: http:// www.youtube.com/watch?v=aNuD0U84NXk

Focal Lesson: Discuss the roles of a recording engineer (oversees the technical aspects of the piece and fixes any problems) and a producer (oversees the creative direction of the piece). Ask students to get into groups of 3-4. One person in the group will be the producer, one will be the engineer and one or two will be the performers.

Each student group will select a piece of poetry from this list: http://www.poets.org/ page.php/prmID/86 to perform.

The producer will take creative lead and suggest how the performers should recite the work. The performers will work together to read the work with attention to line, fluency, and emphasis. Once the group is ready, they can record their recitation using either Garageband (mac) or Audacity (PC). The engineer will listen for any problems and correct via the software tool and may add enhancements as need (background beats or music, etc). The producer will make suggestions and the performers will re-record as needed.

Students will share their a live version of their performance, followed by the recorded/edited version.

| Integrated Assessment and Extension | **Music Mixing Critique**

Ask students to listen to each group perform both the live and edited versions of their poems. The class will complete a rubric analysis of how each group used mixing and mastering to enhance the poem.

Suggested Grade-Band Extensions

K-2: Using grade-level poetry, create compositions using "found sounds" (paper tearing, water bottle crunching, etc) to explore their environment and create a sound poem. Retain the roles, but teacher can record each group performance. Students can make suggestions for editing.

3-5: Using grade-level poetry, create compositions using selected musical instruments such as boomwackers, drums, bells, shakers, etc to convey the poem's intent. Retain the roles from the lesson, but work in station rotations to record the performance with teacher guidance as needed. Students can analyze the performances of their peers and make editing suggestions. Students can edit in a future station rotation.

6-8: Using grade-level poetry, create compositions using selected musical instruments such as boomwackers, drums, bells, shakers, etc to convey the poem's intent. Retain the roles from the lesson, but each group can record and edit their own composition through Audacity or Garageband. Groups can then trade their finished composition to another group who can analyze and edit the original version. Compare and contrast what happens when different producers edit based upon their own vision. |

Reflection Opportunities			
Student Reflection Prompts:	**Key Questions to Ask Students:** 1. What are the roles of engineers? 2. How can we use music to help us engineer the plot of a composition?	Teacher Reflection Prompts:	**Key Questions to Ask Yourself:** 1. Was there a seamless connection between the music and science in this lesson? 2. What pieces of this lesson were a challenge? Which pieces were most engaging for me and my students?

Producing Beats Assessment Rubric

Content Standard Assessed: NGSS **HS-ETS1-4.** Use a computer simulation to model the impact of proposed solutions to a complex real-world problem with numerous criteria and constraints on interactions within and between systems relevant to the problem.

Arts Standards Assessed: MU:Cr1-T.II.a: (Imagine) Explore sounds and compose or improvise multiple musical ideas, excerpts, melodies, or arrangements that exhibit originality, unity and variety for a specific purpose or to express intent, personal interests or experiences using digital tools and resources.

Criteria	Distinguished Level (4)	Excelled Level (3)	Adequate Level (2)	Basic Level (1)
Each student contributes to the project in their assigned role	Producers listen to all elements of the process and facilitate the creative direction of the assignment.

Engineers fix all technical errors and use the various computer software elements to enhance the overall performance.

Performers recite the poem using musical elements and respond to all of the producer's suggestions. | Producers listen to many elements of the process and facilitate the creative direction of the assignment.

Engineers fix most of the technical errors and use the various computer software elements to enhance the overall performance.

Performers recite the poem using musical elements and respond to most of the producer's suggestions. | Producers listen to some elements of the process and facilitate the creative direction of the assignment.

Engineers fix some technical errors and use the various computer software elements to enhance the overall performance.

Performers recite the poem using musical elements and respond to some of the producer's suggestions. | Producers listen to few elements of the process and facilitate the creative direction of the assignment.

Engineers fix few technical errors and use few computer software elements to enhance the overall performance.

Performers recite the poem using few musical elements and respond to few of the producer's suggestions. |

Students use analysis of the text to develop a creative remix of the poem for presentation	Students in the group engage in a discussion and analysis of the text and contribute ideas based upon their evaluation of the text to develop a performance that enhances the overall message.	Students in the group engage in a short discussion and analysis of the text and contribute some ideas based upon their evaluation of the text to develop a performance that enhances the overall message.	Students in the group engage in a short discussion of the text and contribute some ideas based upon their evaluation of the text to develop a performance that enhances the overall message.	Students in the group review the text and contribute few ideas based upon their evaluation of the text to develop a performance that enhances the overall message.

| Students model the impact of computer studio alterations to a recording with mixing and mastering techniques | Performers in the group record their recited poem through the computer software and adjust their performance based upon the producer's suggestions and critiques.

The producer provides clear, specific instructions to the performers and engineer on the alteration of tracks.

The engineer demonstrates exceptional skill in mixing and mastering the recorded track using the computer software to create a performance that highlights the essence of the poem. | Performers in the group record their recited poem through the computer software and adjust much their performance based upon the producer's suggestions and critiques.

The producer provides specific instructions to the performers and engineer on the alteration of tracks.

The engineer demonstrates many skills in mixing and mastering the recorded track using the computer software to create a performance that highlights the essence of the poem. | Performers in the group record their recited poem through the computer software and adjust some their performance based upon the producer's suggestions and critiques.

The producer provides some instructions to the performers and engineer on the alteration of tracks.

The engineer demonstrates some skills in mixing and mastering the recorded track using the computer software to create a performance that highlights the essence of the poem. | Performers in the group record their recited poem through the computer software and do not adjust their performance based upon the producer's suggestions and critiques.

The producer provides few instructions to the performers and engineer on the alteration of tracks.

The engineer demonstrates few skills in mixing and mastering the recorded track using the computer software to create a performance that highlights the essence of the poem. |
|---|---|---|---|---|

Students perform the selected poem in a way that enhances the message of the text.	The performers share a live version of the recitation that deeply showcases their ability to use their voices to communicate the poem's message.	The performers share a live version of the recitation that mostly showcases their ability to use their voices to communicate the poem's message.	The performers share a live version of the recitation that adequately showcases their ability to use their voices to communicate the poem's message.	The performers share a live version of the recitation that weakly showcases their ability to use their voices to communicate the poem's message.
	The producer provides explicit creative details about the final track to share with the class during the presentation.	The producer provides several creative details about the final track to share with the class during the presentation.	The producer provides some creative details about the final track to share with the class during the presentation.	The producer provides few creative details about the final track to share with the class during the presentation.
	The engineer provides rich, explicit details about what was done to alter the original track.	The engineer provides several details about what was done to alter the original track.	The engineer provides some details about what was done to alter the original track.	The engineer provides few details about what was done to alter the original track.

DANCE

Integrated Lesson Plan	Bookmarking Strategy

Content Area: Engineering	Fine Arts Area: Movement	Lesson Title: Decoding DiVinci

Grade Level: 9-12	Duration: (3) 60-90 minute classes	Teacher:

Standards and Alignment

Content Area Standard(s):	Fine Arts Standard(s):
HS-ETS1-4. Use a computer simulation to model the impact of proposed solutions to a complex real-world problem with numerous criteria and constraints on interactions within and between systems relevant to the problem.	Dance: **Artistic Process:** Connecting **Anchor Standard**: Synthesize and relate knowledge and personal experiences to make art.

Big Idea:	Inventing a solution to specific problem	Essential Question:	How are inventions developed?
21st Century Skills:	Creativity, Collaboration, Evaluate Information, Analyze Media, Create Media Product	Key Vocabulary:	DaVinci, invention, code, proportion, structure, function, movement

Vertical Alignment	Before Lesson:	During Lesson:	After Lesson:
	Investigation of current problems in the immediate vicinity that are reasonable to consider for building possible solutions	Using the structures of daVinci's work process to develop computer simulation solution for an identified problem using a common object	Build the computer simulation into a working prototype
Materials List:	Scratch website (scratch.mit.edu), daVinci sketches (http://www.unmuseum.org/leosketch.htm), Flying Machines sketches (http://www.flyingmachines.org/davi.html) pencils, pens, journals, digital cameras/phones, computers, printers		

Instructional Delivery (guided, collaborative, and self-directed)

Student Learning Outcome(s):	I can develop a solution to an existing problem using a computer simulation
Pre-Engagement:	**Pre-assessment:** Ask students to find an ordinary object in the classroom environment, photograph it and sketch it in a visual journal. Pre-assess their ability to accurately depict the object with proper proportion, detail and structure. **Engagement:** Ask students to compare their sketch to the object. Think about ways this object could be more functional or used in a different way. Ask students to write down their ideas using question statements such as "what would happen if…" and "if I changed _____, then _____ ?" Suggest at least one way in which the object could use motion.

Focal Lesson:	Ask students to view examples of daVinci's sketchbooks. Engage in discussions about how daVinci used the arts (including movement) as an avenue to understand and experiment with scientific principles through his sketchbooks.
	Compare daVinci's observations and questions with their own. What is the same? What is different? Focus on his sketches on Flying Machines. What questions are being explored? How did daVinci use traditional mathematical practices to challenge convention and create something new? What elements of motion and movement are being captured in these images? Use the Bookmarking strategy to identify the specific answers to the questions. Bookmark the sequence of steps that daVinci took to prototype the idea of a flying machine.
	Look at the sketches of their own objects and their explorative questions. Challenge students to create a new invention using their original object as inspiration. Use the current structures and form as a framework for their new inventions, and all inventions must be able to move using the elements of space, locomotor or non-locomotor motion, and energy. Create an outline of a process for developing the invention using the sequence they created from the Bookmarking strategy. Students can work in teams or alone.
	Students will share their uncommon "common objects" inventions with the class. Explore how to create these as a prototype using the online programming tool from scratch.mit.edu

| Integrated Assessment and Extension | **Coding Your Invention**

Ask students to upload either the sketch of their item or the digital photograph of their chosen object. Then, using scratch.mit.edu, program their object to function as they intend in their new iteration of this found object. IE: a pen can write by itself based on dictation from a human voice. Create an animation through Scratch coding that demonstrates how the pen will function.

Suggested Grade-Band Extensions

K-2: Instead of focusing on found objects, explore the elements of movement outlined in this lesson and then use the free online app Daisy the Dinosaur to help code Daisy to move using those elements.

3-5: Students can do the same modification as in K-2, but use the scratch.mit.edu website.

6-8: These students can create a game through the scratch.mit.edu website that uses various movement elements to advance through the game portal. |

Reflection Opportunities

| Student Reflection Prompts: | **Key Questions to Ask Students:**
1.What is a prototype and why is it important?
2. How do you define the invention process? | Teacher Reflection Prompts: | **Key Questions to Ask Yourself:**
1. Was there a seamless connection between the movement and technology in this lesson?
2. What pieces of this lesson were a challenge? Which pieces were most engaging for me and my students? |

Decoding daVinci Assessment Rubric

Content Standard Assessed: **HS-ETS1-4.**Use a computer simulation to model the impact of proposed solutions to a complex real-world problem with numerous criteria and constraints on interactions within and between systems relevant to the problem.

Arts Standards Assessed: Dance: **Artistic Process:** Connecting **Anchor Standard**: Synthesize and relate knowledge and personal experiences to make art.

Criteria	Student Response
Does the prototype function as described and/ or intended? (4 points)	Points awarded: Evidence-based response:
Does the prototype utilize locomotor/non-locomotor motion, energy or space in its design? (4 points)	Points awarded: Evidence-based response:
Is the prototype a useful transformation from the original object's function? (4 points)	Points awarded: Evidence-based response:
Based upon your experience in class, please explain the impact this proposed solution will have on a real-world problem. Provide examples to justify your answer. (4 points)	Points awarded: Evidence-based response:

end notes | references

Notes

Chapter 1

Hew, K.F and Brush, T. (2006), *Integrating technology into K-12 teaching and learning: current knowledge gaps and recommendations for future research.* Published online: 5 December 2006, Association for Educational Communications and Technology 2006. Accessed March 21, 2014, http://santersero.pbworks.com/f/Integrating+technology+into+k_12+teaching.pdf

Silverstein, L. B. and Layne, S. (2010), *Defining Arts Integration*, The John F. Kennedy Center for the Performing Arts. Accessed March 21, 2014, http://artsedge.kennedy-center.org/~/media/ArtsEdge/LessonPrintables/articles/arts-integration/DefiningArtsIntegration.pdf

Ingram, D., & Meath, M. (2007). *Arts for academic achievement: A compilation of evaluation findings from 2004-2006.* Center for Applied Research and Educational Improvement.

Mason, C. Y., Steedly, K. M., & Thormann, M. S. (2008). *Impact of arts integration on voice, choice, and access.* Teacher Education and Special Education: The Journal of the Teacher Education Division of the Council for Exceptional Children, 31(1), 36.

Respress, T., & Lutfi, G. (2006). Whole brain learning: The fine arts with students at risk. *Reclaiming Children & Youth*, 15(1), 24-31

Stevenson, L., & Deasy, R. J. (2005). *Third space: When learning matters.* Washington, DC: Arts Education Partnership.

Hardiman, M., Magsamen, S., McKhann, G., and Eilber, J. (2009). *Neuroeducation: Learning, Arts and the Brain.* Dana Press. Accessed March 23, 2014, http://dev.steam-notstem.com/wp-content/uploads/2010/11/Neuroeducation.pdf

Chapter 2

Piney Grove Elementary School, Kernersville, NC. Melissa Edwards, Instructional Technologist. http://www.wsfcs.k12.nc.us/Domain/5196

Chapter 3

Riley, S (2012). Use Arts Integration to Enhance Common Core, Published online Edutopia.org, Accessed March 23, 2014, http://www.edutopia.org/blog/core-practices-arts-integration-susan-riley

Orange County Public Schools (2011). Arts Integration Strategies. https://www.ocps.net/cs/services/cs/currareas/FA/IR/ArtsIntegration/Pages/Arts-Integration-Strategies.aspx

Gray, D., Brown, S., Macanufo, J. (2010). Gamestorming: a Playbook for Innovators, Rulebreakers, and Changemakers. O'Reilly Media, CA.

Donahue, D., Stuart, J. (2010). Artful Teaching: Integrating the Arts for Understanding Across the Curriculum K-8. Teachers College Press, New York, NY and National Art Education Association, Reston, VA.

Ritchhart, R., Church, M., Morrison, K. (2011). Making Thinking Visible: How to Promote Engagement, Understanding and Independence for All Learners. Jossey-Bass, San Francisco, CA.

Chapter 4

Bennett, S., Maton, K. & Kervin, L. (2008) The 'digital natives' debate: a critical review of the evidence, *British Journal of Educational Technology,* 39(5), 775–786.

Bootstrap. *The Algebra Inside your Video Game.* http://www.bootstrapworld.org/AlgebraInsideVideogame.pdf

"Code." Merriam-Webster.com. Merriam-Webster, n.d. Web. 20 Mar. 2014. http://www.merriam-webster.com/dictionary/code

Darling-Hammond, L., Richardson, N. (2009). *Research Review/Teacher Learning: What Matters?* Accessed March 23, 2014 online: http://www.mimathandscience.org/downloads/math_professional_development/how_teachers_learn_20110908_165813_22.pdf

Bouman, K. (2012). *Retention of Learning: Student-led Classrooms or Traditional Classrooms?* Accessed March 23, 2014 online: http://www.smsu.edu/campuslife/learningcommunity/research%20papers/kimboumanpierrelc%20.pdf

Froyd, J., Simpson, N (2010). *Student-Centered Learning Addressing Faculty Questions About Student-Centered Learning.* Accessed March 23, 2014 online: http://ccliconference.org/files/2010/03/Froyd_Stu-CenteredLearning.pdf

Chapter 5

North Elementary School, Cedar City, UT. Melanie Skankey, Arts Integration Specialist. http://north.ironk12.org

ArtsEdge Website Resource, The Kennedy Center. http://artsedge.kennedy-center.org

Chapter 6

UnderArmour Investor Relations, http://investor.underarmour.com/investors.cfm

Lohr, S (2011). *Reaping the Rewards of Risk Taking*. New York Times, Aug 27, 2011: BU3 Accessed March 26, 2014, http://www.nytimes.com/2011/08/28/technology/steve-jobs-and-the-rewards-of-risk-taking.html

Pentland, S. *The New Science of Building Great Teams,* Accessed March 26, 2014, http://hbr.org/2012/04/the-new-science-of-building-great-teams

Sinar, E.F., Wellins, R.S., Pacione, C. (2012). *Creating the Conditions for Sustainable Innovation*, Accessed March 24, 2014. http://www.ddiworld.com/thought-leadership/research/trend-research/creating-the-conditions-for-sustainable-innovation

Corporate Executive Board (2010). *Making the Case for Radical Innovation* Accessed March 24, 2014, http://mlcwideangle.exbdblogs.com/2010/12/08/making-the-case-for-radical-innovation/

Stevens, K. (2002). school as studio: Learning through the arts. Kappa Delta Pi Record, 39(1), 20-23.

OECD (2008), *21st Century Learning: Research, Innovation and Policy*, Paris. Accessed March 26, 2014, http://www.oecd.org/site/educeri21st/ 40554299.pdf

Chapter 7

Walter Bracken STEAM Academy, Las Vegas, NV. Kathryn Decker, Principal. http://schools.ccsd.net/bracken/

Chapter 8

Jacobs, H. H. (Ed.). (1989). *Interdisciplinary curriculum: Design and implementation*. Alexandria, VA: Association for Supervision and Curriculum Development.

Barab, S. A., & Landa, A. (1997). Designing effective interdisciplinary anchors. *Educational Leadership*, 54(6), 52-58.

LaPorte, J., & Sanders, M. (1996). *Technology science mathematics*. New York: Glenco/McGraw-Hill.

150+ Essential Questions for Math, Rowan University. Accessed online March 27, 2014, http://bit.ly/1j90L3l

Daum, K (2005). Entrepreneurs: the artists of the business world. Accessed online March 27, 2014, http://taeinternational.com/Entrepreneurs.pdf

Roach, J. (2013) Teen's invention could charge your phone in 20 seconds. NBC News. Accessed online March 27, 2014, http://www.nbcnews.com/technology/teens-invention-could-charge-your-phone-20-seconds-1C9977955

Part 3

National Governors Association Center for Best Practices & Council of Chief State School Officers. (2010) Common Core State Standards. Washington, DC: Authors. http://corestandards.org

NGSS Lead States. (2013) Next Generation Science Standards: For States, By States. Washington, DC: The National Academies Press. http://nextgenscience.org

International Society for Technology in Education. (2007) ISTE | NETS Student Standards. http://www.iste.org/standards/standards-for-students

National Coalition for Core Arts Standards. (2014) National Core Arts Standards - Draft Documents. Accessed online March 27, 2014, http://nccas.wikispaces.com

about | the author

Susan M. Riley is an arts integration specialist and the CEO of EducationCloset, an online professional development resource for integrated and innovative teaching. She focuses on teacher professional development in arts integration, STEAM, and Common Core State Standards through the arts. A nationally-recognized consultant and author, her work has been featured by Americans for the Arts, EducationWeek and Edutopia.

VISIONYST Press
an imprint of The Vision Board, LLC

Discover. Explore.
CREATE.

Additional resources for STEAM:

STEAM point. *The original STEAM workbook from Susan M. Riley!*

Shake the Sketch. *A process-based guide for implementing arts integration successfully at any school.*

JOIN US in an online community for the arts!

* Free daily articles
* Annual conference
* Online, graduate-level classes

VISIT US at educationcloset.com

CPSIA information can be obtained at www.ICGtesting.com
Printed in the USA
BVOW05s1424140516

447684BV00007B/123/P